THE BAPTIST DEACON

ROBERT E. NAYLOR

THE
BAPTIST
DEACON

BROADMAN PRESS
Nashville, Tennessee

Copyright, 1955
BROADMAN PRESS
Nashville, Tennessee

ISBN: 0-8054-3501-8
4235-01

PRINTED IN THE UNITED STATES OF AMERICA

CONTENTS

INTRODUCTION:
THE DEACON AND I

M en are more important than battles, so far as modern historians are concerned. Various approaches can be taken in writing history from the biographical point of view, and I believe that I could write the story of my life or have it told by another in terms of deacons. From my earliest recollection, many of the men who have molded my life or made great contribution to it have served as deacons in Baptist churches. Thus deacons are more important than events in my experience. Even then, I naturally ask myself, "Why should I talk about deacons? Do I have any particular qualifications which would enable me to share something worthwhile about this matter?" As I have thought about it, I believe that there are at least three basic things in my life and experience that would have value in a discussion of deacons.

Childhood experiences.—First of all, I am the son of a Baptist preacher. Born in a parsonage in the early days of Oklahoma's statehood, my earliest recollections are of a preacher's household and a pastorate in a pioneer state. I have had deacons for breakfast, dinner, and supper as far back as I can remember. At mealtime, Dad and Mother would discuss the affairs of the day and the people of the church, careful always to keep their conversation on that which the children ought to hear. Among the precious memories that are mine are certain names and faces, most of them now with their Lord, that meant a great deal to me as the son of the pastor. Let me tell about two of the many deacons who meant so much in my childhood.

One deacon in Dad's church of that early day was a full-blood Choctaw Indian. There came a time in our family when Mother was very, very sick. This deacon, a man of few words, came to see my father and indicated that he would like to talk to him privately. The parsonage was new, the first two-story house in which we had ever lived. The men went upstairs together. Later, I heard Dad tell Mother what had happened. The deacon, a man of some means, got out a checkbook and handed it to my father without a word. Dad opened it. The first check was signed, but the amount was yet to be filled in. This was true of every check in the book. With tears running down his face, the deacon had simply said, "Wife sick, need money, help youself." Could I forget him? Never.

There was another early deacon who meant quite a bit to me in a different way. Dad got a notion one time that a boy couldn't be properly reared unless he was on a farm. I didn't believe in that philosophy at all, but it was such a fixation with Dad that he decided to resign his church and move us to the farm. One Sunday morning, he arose and wept as he offered his resignation. The congregation wept, and I sat there in fear. He had bought ninety acres of government land down on the river, new virgin land that he had cleared himself. He wanted me to pile brush on that land. Towards the back of the crowded church a deacon stood up. He had not been very active in the church, but he looked as if he had a broken heart. He said, "Pastor, I just don't believe that it is of God. I don't believe God is in it. I, for one, am not willing to accept it." My dad was a man of decided opinions and convictions, but this deacon persuaded him. I haven't ceased to be grateful.

Besides these men, many other deacons stand out in my

memory of boyhood days for the influence that their Christian characters had on my life.

Deacons in the Bible.—I would not lay claim to unusual scholarship, and what I know about deacons as they are presented in the Bible is known by many preachers. I am sure that there are more things in the Book than I know, yet I am grateful to God for the opportunity to make a reverent examination of his truth. I believe that my conviction about the Bible is a qualification for writing about deacons. Not only do I believe that all of the Bible is true, that it is the Word of God, but I believe that the patterns and programs that it presents are timeless in their significance and effectiveness. This means that the office of deacon as presented in the Bible makes that office necessary in our churches.

Regardless of how much deacons meant in my early experience, I do not believe that an approach based merely on past values warrants a full-length discussion of the office. That which may have been very wonderful in years gone by may not be of immediate moment. The timeless quality of the office comes from the fact that God himself has seen fit to establish it in the churches and to give positive instructions about it in the Scriptures. A right approach to the subject must consider its meaning for the churches in the twentieth century. God has given a revelation about an office that is for the twentieth century and its needs.

Deacons in my ministry.—Some essential qualifications for writing about deacons come from twenty-five years in the Baptist ministry, pastoring churches large and small. In these churches there have been groups of deacons whom I have loved, men who have done great things for God.

In my first pastorate after leaving the seminary, I had a coffee salesman as a deacon who was the greatest soul winner in the church, without exception. His trips on the road were used as opportunities to talk to people about Jesus. He taught a group of young men in Sunday school and, needless to say, did a good job of it.

We had a sixteen-year-old class of boys that we were losing (as classes are sometimes lost at that age), and something had to be done. I went to this deacon friend and said, "Brother Charlie, we are going to lose this class unless someone helps us. I know how your boys love you, and I know what you are doing with them, but I am asking you as your preacher to turn loose of that class and take charge of these other boys. I believe it is the most critical thing in our church now."

He answered, "Whatever the pastor asks me to do, I'll do."

The next Sunday, he began his work with those boys. Only two or three weeks later, he took them out rabbit hunting at night. They went in a truck and hunted by the headlights. As they were coming back, one of the boys who was riding on the cab was knocked to the bottom of the truck by a bump in the road. His gun went off, and this deacon friend was killed. It was three o'clock in the morning when I was called and told about it. It seemed that the end of the world had come for me. Even now, I rarely get up to preach without thinking of Charlie Holt and his faithful testimony for the Lord.

A lawyer deacon whom I had known in a later pastorate wrote me a letter, telling how a friend had given him a newspaper containing a sermon which I had preached to my congregation at the time. He said, "I have read the sermon very carefully. I want you to tell your wife that I believe that she is doing better with her sermon writing as you go along." How I enjoyed that! To tell of all the wonderful things which this man did in his church, of the things which he contributed to my ministry, would take half a book in itself.

These things should emphasize the fact that the subject of deacons is very sacred to me. It is out of such experiences and preparation that the outline for this book has emerged, a book dealing with a life that God has signally blessed through an office that he instituted. The many men who have served faithfully in this office form a noble company. Individually, they have honored God, advanced the kingdom, and strengthened the ministry of some pastor. My own ministry has really been the deacon and I.

ARE DEACONS NEEDED NOW?

After spending a week in Virginia speaking to deacons, I received a letter from the wife of a deacon in a country Baptist church. She had read of our deacons' school in the state Baptist paper and wanted to know if there was a real reason for the continuance of the office. Was there any particular service which a deacon could render in a country church where the number of members was small? She indicated that her husband was a faithful Christian in their church but that his being a deacon meant nothing. In answering, I assured her that the office of deacon is scriptural and when rightly understood, presents a real opportunity for service.

How much does the office of deacon mean in the reader's church? What would be the effect upon its program if, by common consent and with a spirit of harmony, the office were abolished next week? In many Baptist churches the actual termination of the office would be a mere formality. Possibly, there are some churches that would welcome the change. A large number of deacons and pastors think that our churches would be better served by other church officers and committees. These men are not heretics or reactionaries but in the greater part, are those honestly seeking to advance the kingdom of God.

In a meeting with another group of pastors and deacons, I invited questions. One pastor asked, "Does a church without a program need deacons?" I hope that he was not referring to his own church. The question is more of an in-

dictment of pastoral leadership than anything else. The main
consideration is that the question is being widely asked. An
indignant shrug is an inadequate answer. The situations
which have produced the question should be carefully
weighed. An honest, intelligent, and scriptural answer ought
to be given.

WHY RAISE THE QUESTION?

The changed world.—What are the conditions which
have caused thinking people to raise the question of the
need for deacons? First of all, there is a staggering contrast
between the world of the first century and that of the twentieth. It is a far cry from the world in which that first church
decided that there was a need for men to serve tables to the
world which is the field of churches today. The tempo has
vastly increased. The complexity of life is reflected in the
churches. The growth of great cities, the growth of churches
both in size and number, the multiplicity of church organizations, and the outreaching services which churches desire
to give, all call for modern methods, streamlined organizations, and increasing efficiency. It is easy to be confused
about the place of deacons in such a world.

Office misunderstood.—In many places the office and
service of deacons is ill defined and little understood. The
average Baptist would have the haziest kind of idea about
what a deacon ought to do. What does the office of deacon
mean in the church? What is the responsibility of the deacon? What is his function? If deacons are needed now, a
reappraisal of the service which they ought to render is also
needed. In Richmond, Virginia, while I was engaged in a
revival meeting, I was asked to spend Saturday evening with
the deacons discussing their function and service in the light
of the New Testament. Since there were no Saturday services, the meeting was meant to be an evening of fellowship

as well. The discussion, which I had intended to last about thirty minutes, went on, by their insistence, more than two hours. I was amazed at the eagerness of these men to know what they were supposed to do in the office which they held. Late in the discussion, one man said, "Say, if I had known all this before I became a deacon, I wouldn't be one." The office and consequent responsibility in this case had been poorly defined. No wonder an intelligent man in such a situation would question the need for deacons.

Leadership tensions.—There is another occasion for the question of need being raised. Tension between pastor and deacons is no uncommon experience in churches. Often this has come to open warfare, and the resulting tragedy has crippled the influence and work of such churches. Some pastors feel that they cannot work through their deacons. They have been heard to say, "I know what I will do. If my deacons will not go along with me, I will take it to the church and let the congregation decide." That situation is spiritually unhealthy.

There is a church in Oklahoma whose pastor decided that the New Testament does not teach that there ought to be deacons. With the consent of the church, he abolished the office—a sizable undertaking for one preacher! The underlying cause was an area of disagreement between deacons and preacher. In a world on fire, Baptists cannot afford to dissipate their energies and weaken their witness with such tensions. If an organization is the cause, then perhaps that organization is not needed.

There are churches where deacons have appropriated to themselves authority which is contrary to New Testament teaching. It may have gone so far that "bossism" has developed. There is a "board" complex and a general feeling that deacons are "directors" of the church. Nothing could be farther from the Baptist genius or the New Testament plan.

Anywhere this condition exists, there inevitably are those who say that deacons are not needed. The truth is that such deacons as this or such organizations are not needed in churches.

Many others who serve.—Although the problems which have just been discussed do not exist in every church (and not all of them in any one church), there is a positive thing which demands a reappraisal of the deacon as an officer in the church. In modern churches, there are many people who hold responsible positions. They teach Sunday school classes, administer departments, lead Training Unions, work in the missionary organizations, sing in the choirs, and do many other vital things. These workers are often required to spend much more time with their tasks than the deacons are. In large city churches, the number of elected people may be in excess of five hundred besides those elected by classes or units and those serving by appointment. In these same churches, the number of deacons is often less than fifty.

Is there a need for an office that gives honor to a few when the vast majority of the people who do the work of the churches do not serve in this office? Deacons certainly are no more deserving of honor than these others, yet they are set aside to a particular honor for a nonparticular service. It is a matter of record that one publication recommends that everybody who holds office in the church, man or woman, should be made a deacon. Such a suggestion sounds ridiculous to most Baptists, but the reasoning behind it is very plain. Odious comparisons are being made in the minds of many people between the group known as deacons and the rest of the active workers in the church.

The difficulties are real, and the problem of this chapter cannot be ignored. People are raising questions about the need for the office. The spiritual health of the churches demands an answer. Most Baptists feel that the office of deacon is an inseparable part of Baptist life, but the reasons should be plain, concise, scriptural, and practical.

DEACONS ARE NEEDED NOW!

Are deacons needed now? Yes! This is the unequivocal answer and becomes the first main premise of this book. Deacons are needed in churches today just as much as they were needed in that first church at Jerusalem. The right understanding and use of the office of deacon provides an answer to many vital problems that confront churches and hamper advance.

Deacons a New Testament pattern.—The chief reason for the conviction that deacons are needed now should be stated first, for everything else is related to it. Deacons are needed now because the office is an inseparable part of the New Testament church pattern. "New Testament pattern" is a phrase that should be particularly meaningful to us Baptists, who like to call our churches New Testament churches and assert that we would not hold membership in any other kind of church. It is our firm conviction that a church should discover its doctrines, determine its organization, define its procedures, and catch its commission in the pages of the New Testament. The program of the church will be formulated in harmony with the teachings of the Book. Saying "New Testament pattern" means much.

The plain teaching of the New Testament should be enough to determine the doctrines and practices of Baptist churches. No other reason for any belief or practice should be necessary. Thus following the pattern of the New Testament is of first importance for all of the church, even its organizations. This conviction is basic in an evaluation of the office of deacon. It even calls for a willingness to examine the Baptist position to be sure of its complete accord with the Word of God. The leadership of the Holy Spirit gave rise to the office of deacon in the New Testament churches. Divine wisdom brought deacons into being, and divine ends were to be accomplished. While the office may be misinterpreted and its usefulness nullified, God has put it into the pattern for a purpose, a purpose that should be discovered and accepted because of its eternal significance.

Is such acceptance of an office mere traditionalism? Not at all! Three things are true of the New Testament church which will be significant in studying this office. First, such a church roots in a relationship, the relationship of a saved sinner to a holy God through Christ Jesus. The church is not first a fellowship but a relationship, its foundation stone being a personal confession of faith in Jesus. In the second place, it is an organization that underlines a responsibility to God. Finally, its divine origin makes its significance and usefulness eternal. God's programs, plans, and strategy are never outdated or outmoded.

What are the historical facts to be considered? Remember the storms that surrounded the first church in Jerusalem. The Jews seemed to have been convinced that the death of Jesus would settle their problems. They thought that his followers would soon disband since their Leader was dead. It was not long, however, until they discovered that there was new leadership provided by the certainty of the disciples that they had been with Jesus. They testified that through resurrection, Christ was alive. Pentecost came and with it the power of God and the growth of the church.

Persecution was the inevitable aftermath. James, the brother of John, was martyred. Peter and John were put in jail and released only after warnings against continued preaching. The disciples only prayed for boldness, and their witness increased. Peter was put in jail, sentenced to death, and miraculously delivered by the angel of God while the church was praying for his deliverance. The raging storms outside the church only kindled the flame of Christian witnessing. In the eighth chapter of Acts it is written, "And at that time there was a great persecution against the church which was at Jerusalem. . . . Therefore they that were scattered abroad went every where preaching the word" (Acts 8:1b, 4). Storms outside can do little damage to a church.

Storms within a church, however, have infinite power to do harm and limit its effective witness. Just such a storm began to develop in the Jerusalem church. It grew out of the problem of taking care of the widows, orphans, and needy. The Grecian members of the church insisted that the Hebrew widows were getting more than their fair share; at this point, the Holy Spirit suggested a solution to the twelve. This was to select seven men of a certain quality and assign to them these problems of distribution. By intimation, the seven were set apart for any other needs for which the church wished to call them. "Then the twelve called the multitude of the disciples unto them and said, It is not reason that we should leave the word of God, and serve tables. Wherefore, brethren, look ye out among you seven men whom we may appoint over this business. But we will give ourselves continually to prayer, and to the ministry of the word" (Acts 6:2–4).

These seven men are not called deacons in the book of Acts. They are most often referred to as "the seven." It is a matter of general agreement, however, that the election of these seven qualified men is the real beginning of the deacon as a church officer. It is in the third chapter of First Timothy that the qualifications of the men who serve as deacons are carefully outlined, while Paul introduced his epistle to the Philippians, "Paul and Timotheus, the servants of Jesus Christ, to all the saints in Christ Jesus which are at Philippi

8 THE BAPTIST DEACON

with the bishops and deacons" (Phil. 1:1). This is a solid scriptural basis for the assumption that, beginning in the Jerusalem church, the office of deacon had developed with the approval and blessing of the Holy Spirit.

A distinction must be drawn between the work that a deacon does and the office that he holds. Overlooking this distinction has caused many misconceptions about deacons, for there is no work that is done exclusively by deacons, no work in which no one else may share. The distinction between the work and the position goes back to the New Testament, where the Greek word translated "deacon" (*diakonos*) is also translated as "minister" and "servant." In the majority of its uses, it does not refer to someone who holds a definite office or position in the church, yet the existence of such an office can be clearly seen in Philippians 1:1, and 1 Timothy 3:8 and 3:12.[1] The New Testament thus uses the same word to describe Christians generally as servants and also a particular officer set aside for service. The deacon has a special responsibility for service, but he serves in the same way that all Christians are called on to serve.

Since the office existed then by the wisdom of God, the discontinuance of the office should not even be considered without express instructions from him. What is needed is a rediscovery of the office, a new exploration of the Scriptures concerning it, and a new committal to the purpose of God in its creation. The New Testament really provides the ade-

[1] Of the thirty occurrences of the work *diakonos* in the Greek New Testament, "minister" is the English translation in twenty cases. An examination of such passages as Matthew 20:26, Romans 13:4 and 15:8, and 1 Timothy 4:6 will reveal that the deacon as an officer of the church is not being discussed. Compare Romans 16:1 and John 2:5 for two out of the seven passages in which the translation is "servant." *Diakonia* is a related noun generally meaning "service" in the New Testament but never referring to the service of a specific officer of the church. The related verb, *diakoneo* ("to serve"), is used thirty-eight times. In 1 Timothy 3:10 and 13, the service of a specific officer is indicated. In other uses, the emphasis is on a more general Christian activity of service and dedication.

quate answer to the question of the need for deacons now. Deacons were needed in New Testament times, and they are needed now.

Nevertheless, there are more specific reasons for having deacons, although these are also related to the Bible. While the particular crisis of the Jerusalem church does not exist in churches today, there are the same principles of crisis. Those men were called to do the type of thing in their church that needs doing in every church by such a dedicated group of men.

Freeing the ministers.—The seven were chosen that they might free the apostles to prayer and the ministry of the word. As a preacher, I always set up a loud cheer in my heart when I read this. If there is any way that deacons can set preachers free, not so much "free from" as "free to" do certain things, it certainly needs to be done now. If it was needed with the simplified church organizations then existing, how much more ministers need to be set free today! In any church nowadays, a pastor can spend all of his time with administration and the extracurricular activities thrust upon him. In the larger church, administering the staff is at least a forty-hour job. The "must" visitation could consume an equal amount of time. Then there are the conference periods that are necessary but endless. Where is the time for prayer, meditation, Bible study, or sermon preparation?

In the last national census, the census taker was instructed to get the usual information, such as the number in the family, ages, and occupations. But about every seventh call, he was supposed to ask for special information. I came home one day to lunch, and my wife said that the census taker had been there. She added that he had asked what seemed to her a good many unnecessary questions. Among other things, he asked, "How many hours does your husband work each week?" I knew that the week had been a little rougher than usual, and so I laughed and asked her what she had told him. Her answer was, "eighty-four hours a week." Maybe the census people are still trying to figure out how a minister works more than one day per week! Anyway, a pastor's wife would vote for a group within the church that could set the minister free to his major ministry.

The function and office of the pastor was not changed when the office of deacon was created. God in his wisdom simply gave to the pastor some of the most wonderful assistance that is to be had in this world. The best illustration is a hand attached to the body to perform the normal functions of the body. The difference is that the deacon is not like a hand that can be commanded but one that must accept its function and operate. The pastor does not command the deacon; he confides in him and relies implicitly upon his service.

The things which the deacon is to do are things which still belong to the area of pastoral leadership. In the performance of these duties, however, God has created another officer that assumes the detailed execution which would absorb the pastor's thought, time, and life. It is taken for granted that the pastor will desire to be acquainted with all that is being done in the church. Recognizing his leadership and seeking his counsel is made desirable by the Scripture. Such a relationship can exist because pastor and deacons share the new nature imparted by Christ. There is no freedom like the freedom of perfect confidence in another. Love at one time binds and sets free. Surely the strongest pastor in the world is that man who has absolute faith in God and absolute faith in the men given to him of God for the execution and the enlargement of his ministry. Thank God for an office in the New Testament church that makes one minister many ministers in his effectiveness for the Lord.

Promoters of church harmony.—Another need met by these seven men in the sixth chapter of Acts was that they became protectors and promoters of church harmony. How serious the breach in fellowship had become in the Jerusalem church is not certain. The expression "a murmuring" is dramatic enough. Someone was needed to pour oil on the troubled waters. These deacons were God's answer, and they healed the breach and restored the fellowship. This work of the seven is not to be forgotten. Unfortunately, deacons do not always serve thus in modern churches. Sometimes a faction in the church is "deacon led."

When a man becomes a deacon, he loses the privilege, if such exists, of participating in a church row. A member in the ranks may claim that often abused privilege, "speaking his mind." When a man becomes a deacon—selected and called by the Holy Spirit, chosen by a church, dedicated by personal choice—he forfeits the right to promote, in any fashion, a division in the life of the church.

The one inescapable duty of the deacon in the New Testament was the protection of the church fellowship. When things arise that are divisive, it is time for a deacon who believes the Book to stand up and say: "We cannot do it this way in this church. We must have harmony and peace if we are to honor Christ." That could make the difference between a great, fruitful church and an ineffective, dried-up one. If deacons were needed then for such harmony, they surely are needed now. The kind of world in which church fellowship must thrive demands deacons.

The welfare of the membership.—Another objective in the election of that first seven was provision for the welfare of the church membership. These men were to undergird the ministry in that particular type of service. Modern church constituencies have multiple needs that often escape the attention of the pastor or are beyond his physical strength. Deacons can render a wonderful service in this area. There should be no forgotten men or women on the church roll. Deacons are needed for this service now.

More effective witness.—It is very evident that this system was established and these seven elected in order that the church might give a more effective witness. That should be the real test for all the church program. In the case of the deacons, the plan worked and thus gave evidence of the divine wisdom that was in it. "And the word of God increased; and the number of the disciples multiplied in Jerusalem greatly; and a great company of the priests were obedient to the faith" (Acts 6:7). Not only does that tell of the necessity for deacons in the churches, but it makes a divine promise to that church which will guard and rightly use the office.

Stronger leadership.—The great over-all justification for the office of deacon was its creation to make a contribution to the effective force of leadership. Why are churches no more effective than they are? It is because of the caliber of their leadership. Some deacon may insist that he is not a leader, that he was born to work behind the scenes; but God makes it abundantly clear that the primary business of the deacon is to add force and effectiveness to leadership.

Of course, all deacons do not lead. There are different degrees of leadership ability, but all degrees are subject to development in force and excellence. The movement of leadership is forward, yet I have known deacons who dragged their feet and always exercised the backstrap. They seemed to feel that it was their special assignment to keep things from moving too fast, apparently on the theory that someone has to object. In a church where I once served, people still tell of a former deacon who is now dead. They said that he was very faithful in his attendance but almost deaf, so that he could hear very little of what was said.

(That can be a blessing on occasions!) This particular brother always found a prominent place in the meeting, and though he could not hear, would arise to say, "Now, brethren, I want you to know that I am again' it." Unfortunately, many who serve as deacons, though they are not hard of hearing, partake of that spirit.

God has surely done a marvelous thing in establishing the office of deacon in the New Testament church. As a pastor, I do not know what I would do if I had to face the responsibilities of a modern church without deacons. I believe that this office was born in the mind and heart of God and that he expects deacons now to add immeasurably to the force of leadership in the churches and the advancement of his kingdom. The needs met by those seven in the first century are twentieth-century needs. It is a supreme privilege to be a part of meeting those needs.

Deacons are needed! There is one way to make the world understand that need and that is a demonstration of what a deacon ought to be. Churches need a holy re-evaluation of this office, including a new understanding of its possibilities and its work. Men who occupy the office must have a new conviction that it is the work of God, with the humility which such a conviction brings. Are deacons needed now? Yes, more than ever, they are needed.

II

QUALIFICATIONS FOR DEACONS

Since the work of the deacon is so vital, what kind of men are adequate for it? Obviously not just anybody will do, for a church is a spiritual concern. Spiritual qualifications are basic, and many present problems have come about from ignoring this. The Scriptures will provide the answer, and the answer found should be carefully followed. But before considering these Scriptural qualifications, a word of caution is necessary.

The qualities ascribed to deacons in the Scriptures are not found exclusively in deacons. For example, the New Testament teaches that deacons ought to be grave, yet they are not the only ones in the church who should be grave. Every man who could be described as being grave is not automatically qualified to be a deacon, but every deacon ought somehow to match the quality which that word "grave" describes.

On the other hand, no deacon has all of the biblical qualities brought to perfection. A man reading the requirements concerning deacons laid down in the Scripture might say to himself, "I feel my shortcomings; I feel entirely unworthy of that." However, preachers cannot read the New Testament as it speaks of God's expectation for a preacher and not feel ashamed, unworthy, and inadequate. The same would be true of deacons. Still it is true that these qualities that the Scriptures present as a part of the life of the deacon ought to be found in all of the men who are set aside to the office.

A church is foolish to expect to find perfect men to fill the office of deacon. Perfection is an expected realization in heaven, not something that is attained here in the life of churches. Earnest people who really love the Lord are very foolish to decline office "because they are not good enough." They will never get any better by declining opportunities to serve Christ and his people. It can be confidently expected that a sincere, saved man who has a degree of these requirements will grow in grace as he serves.

Now let the Scripture speak to the church about the kind of men it will look for in selecting deacons. Let it speak to the men so serving about the kind of men they must be to fulfil their obligation. Although the seven men in the sixth chapter of Acts are not called deacons, it is generally accepted that this is the place of beginning. The qualities desired of them are surely to be desired of deacons now. The other related passage, which definitely describes the office, is found in the third chapter of First Timothy.

THE PATTERN OF THE SEVEN

Wherefore, brethren, look ye out among you seven men of honest report, full of the Holy Ghost and wisdom, whom we may appoint over this business. But we will give ourselves continually to prayer, and to the ministry of the word.

And the saying pleased the whole multitude: and they chose Stephen, a man full of faith and of the Holy Ghost, and Philip, and Prochorus, and Nicanor, and Timon, and Parmenas, and Nicolas a proselyte of Antioch: whom they set before the apostles: and when they had prayed, they laid their hands on them. And the word of God increased; and the number of the disciples multiplied in Jerusalem greatly; and a great company of the priests were obedient to the faith. And Stephen, full of faith and power, did great wonders and miracles among the people (Acts 6:3–8).

These verses form the first significant passage of Scripture

about the deacon. There are several characteristics which
can be studied in detail.

Honest report.—First of all, a deacon ought to be of
"honest report." The word that is translated "honest report"
is very interesting. The Greek word in the New Testament
which is translated "witness" and from which the English
word "martyr" comes is related to it. The word here in Acts
means that men witness good things about one.[1] Whatever a
man may say about himself, if people outside the church
cannot or will not say good things about him, his potentialities as a deacon are doubtful. There is something blame-
worthy in a man's character if the consensus of opinion is
unfavorable to him, no matter how much he may be admired
and respected by his own party. There may be times when it
is all right to defy public opinion, but it does not follow that
the objection of the world makes a thing right. Men who are
selected as deacons in the church ought to be those about
whom the consensus of opinion is good.

Full of the Holy Ghost.—The seven men of Acts 6 were to
be "full of the Holy Ghost and wisdom." The word "full" occurs in other significant passages of Scripture: Stephen was
"full of faith and power"; Luke said that Jesus was "full of
the Holy Ghost" (Luke 4:1); John said that the Word was
"full of Grace and Truth" (1:14); Barnabas was "full of the
Holy Ghost and of faith" (Acts 11:24). What does fulness
of the Holy Ghost or of spiritual virtues mean? Does it refer
to quantity—"three quarts of faith"—or to quality, as the

---

[1] The word is used twenty-five times in the New Testament meaning "to
bear witness." The eleventh chapter of Hebrews says that the elders obtained "a good report," meaning that people said good things about them.
The same chapter speaks of those who "through faith obtained a good
report." *A Greek-English Lexicon of the New Testament* by Joseph Henry
Thayer indicates that the word means "to affirm that one has seen or heard
or experienced something." The passive voice, as used in Acts 6:3, means
"to be well reported of, to have (good) testimony borne to one, accredited,
attested, of good report, approved" (pp. 390–391) .

spirit of sincerity and zeal? Mostly the latter, I think. The word "full" (*pleres*) means "covered in every part, thoroughly permeated with, complete, lacking nothing." [2] It represents wholeheartedness, total sincerity, complete dedication.

For the deacon, it is an admonition to bigness. No man ought to serve as deacon who is little and pinched and dwarfed in his spiritual outlook or personal dedication. Mr. Little-faith or Little-spirit or Little-wisdom would make a very poor deacon. Littleness, for the want of a better word, is the curse of any church where ever it is found in the membership. Its destructive hurt is greater in potential than many of the more frowned-on sins. But in leadership, it is absolutely ruinous, a deadly foe to progress in the kingdom of God. God deliver us from little men, preachers or deacons. As suggested in the beginning, being little need not characterize any man that desires to be otherwise. Growth in grace is one of the marvels of redemption. Little men can become big by the grace of God.

Much could be written here about the Holy Ghost or Holy Spirit. A multitude of books have been written about him. Christians know that he is God with them, the third person in the Trinity. He comes into the heart of the believer at the moment of saving faith and is the Agent who works the miracle of the new birth. His business is to convict the world of sin, righteousness, and judgment. He is to make real to Christian minds and hearts all things concerning Jesus. To be "full of him" is to be wholly yielded to his direction. The Holy Spirit in full possession of the Christian brings holiness to life and the power of God to works.

These men who served as deacons were to be spiritual men. (Be careful of that word "spiritual," for the Book mentions spiritual wickedness. Some people speak of a person as

[2] Thayer's *Lexicon*, p. 517.

being "spiritual" because he seems to have a pretentious type of piety that repels more than it attracts.) True spirituality is not first an attitude or act but a relationship to the Holy Spirit. I cannot imagine a person's being genuinely spiritual in this sense without being tremendously attractive and winsome.

Not much is said here about the secular abilities or business qualifications of these men. That is largely taken for granted and will be considered a little later. The great emphasis is upon spiritual means. As a Bible study exercise, read the biographies of those described as being "full of the Spirit." It is a challenge to a man to be more than he is by the power of God. It is a challenge to a church to seek out men for this office who are willing to be possessed of the Spirit. The initial experience of grace is presumed, for no person can be spiritual in whom the Holy Spirit does not abide. This is the demand for total dedication, for surrender of self and all, to the personal presence of God.

Full of wisdom.—Deacons should be full of wisdom. That word does not exclude common sense, but in the New Testament, it always takes its flavor from the setting in which it is found. It occurs fifty-one times. Luke's word is often quoted concerning the childhood of Jesus, "Jesus increased in wisdom" (2:52). Paul called Christ "the wisdom of God" (1 Cor. 1:24). There is comfort in James' word, "If any of you lack wisdom, let him ask of God, that giveth to all men liberally" (1:5). The shade of meaning in each particular case is described by its context.

The wisdom of deacons can be compared to that possession of a man by the Spirit just discussed. It is wisdom born in a relationship. Men act and choose wisely when they are wisely led. This does not mean that the deacon has to be a learned man. Learned men are not necessarily wise men. The life and ministry of any man should be fuller and richer for real learning, but the wisdom required here is essentially of a high spiritual order. In the first responsibility committed to these seven, wisdom of this kind was a necessity; and the success of the enterprise was largely due to it.

Full of faith.—Deacons should be full of faith. This is not stated directly as a requirement but is an inference drawn from the choice of Stephen who was a man full of faith. Dr. B. H. Carroll offered the opinion that it meant that Stephen had a clearer and stronger faith than any other man then living on the earth. No one of the apostles had such clear recognition of the meaning of the kingdom of God and of the church and its work as this man Stephen. Certain it is that he was a colossal figure in the history of the early church, and his being full of faith is the explanation. This is the direction in which men selected as deacons should move. They ought to be possessed of a great wisdom concerning the kingdom of God and the main business of his church. This will put the emphasis of their life and service in the right place.

Since these first deacons were full of the Holy Ghost and of wisdom and of faith, it is axiomatic that they were also full of power. In the story of Stephen's preaching and his controversy and debate with the high priest and the council, it is said, "They were not able to resist the wisdom and the spirit by which he spake" (Acts 6:10). The man was simply irresistible when clothed with the Spirit and filled with faith. The debate had probably been suggested by his enemies and the challenge accepted by Stephen. They brought in the best talent that they had. Finally false witnesses were summoned. The force of righteousness had to be reckoned with. Stephen met every argument and overcame it. Their anger was occasioned by their defeat. They killed Stephen because they could not stop him any other way. It was a confession of defeat.

A deacon that gets harnessed properly to God's Spirit and his program and purpose is a force to be reckoned with. If all of the deacons in all of the churches could be possessed with a conviction that God has something for them to do and say, if they could have a sense of a responsibility to meet and of being men of the hour for God, it would turn the world upside down. I learned long ago the strength of total deacon enlistment in my pastorates. If deacons, placed in their position of God and selected by the church, are committed to a New Testament program in their church under the Spirit of God, the church will move forward. Stephen got results and so will any deacon so dedicated. The man with aspirations to be another Stephen can count on God's help. He can be sure of power. He can be sure of achieving for the kingdom of God. It may cost dearly, as it cost Stephen. Do not lose sight of the fact that deacons tied to the will of God are mighty in their power with God and with men.

Businessmen.—The deacons should have certain secular qualifications. These receive minor treatment in the Scriptures; but because of the things they were to do, it was taken for granted that they would represent the best of human leadership. The instruction in the selection of the seven was that they should be men who could be appointed "over this business." It is very plain that a new rank of ministerial orders was not being created but that secular responsibilities were being distributed. If too much is not made of the modern meaning of the term, it is safe to say that these seven were businessmen.

The word "business" should be discussed a little to prevent any misunderstanding. The Greek word is *chreia* and basically means "need." It is so translated twenty-five times. This is the only place that it is translated "business." Hence there is no scriptural authority for the deacons to make the financial decisions of the church. Church decisions must remain *church* decisions. I heard a deacon quote the passage in a deacons' meeting as proof that the finance committee should consist only of deacons. The nature of the deacons' work in the business of the church will be discussed in Chapter VII. It is good to select men of practical business judgment and experience as deacons. This is a minor though not unimportant qualification. The chief requirements are spiritual. The deacon is a servant of the church. His life is to be matched against the needs of the members. It is certainly desirable and an advantage if he possesses a leadership ability and an effective know-how. Capable men can be spiritual men.

QUALIFICATIONS IN FIRST TIMOTHY

The third chapter of First Timothy presents a new list of deacon qualifications. It is worth noting that the preacher's qualifications are listed first, giving form and emphasis to the deacon list. The two offices are clearly established, and only qualified men are to serve. Every minister and every deacon will want to measure himself against these requirements and seek improvement. Look at the requirements for deacons:

Likewise must the deacons be grave, not doubletongued, not given to much wine, not greedy of filthy lucre; holding the mystery of faith in a pure conscience. And let these also first be proved; then let them use the office of a deacon, being found blameless. Even so must their wives be grave, not slanderers, sober, faithful in all things. Let the deacons be the husbands of one wife, ruling their children and their own houses well. For they that have used the office of a deacon well purchase to themselves a good degree, and great boldness in the faith which is in Christ Jesus (1 Tim. 3:8–13).

In these verses, there are both negative and positive qualities. In looking at the negative qualities first, it must be remembered that a deacon cannot be made from negative material. Merely quitting certain things does not make one pleasing to God. The fact that a man quits swearing does not mean that he has become a Christian. He becomes a little more respectable but not necessarily regenerated. As someone has said, when a man quits "chewing," he becomes more sanitary, but it does not necessarily follow that he has become a Christian.

There is a picture in the Scripture of a man's life as compared to a house that had been swept and garnished, with all of the devils cast out. When nothing was brought in to fill the empty place, the devils came back seven times as strong as before. A Christian cannot be made by negation. What First Timothy is saying about deacons is that there are certain things which ought not to be a part of a deacon's life. Men who have such things present and not corrected in their lives must not be made deacons.

Not doubletongued.—Paul wrote Timothy that a deacon is not to be doubletongued. This is the only place in the Scripture where this word is found. It means saying one thing to one person and something else to another. There are men that would say one thing before one audience and another thing before a different one. Such a man is doubletongued. The word as used in the Scripture is unfavorable, for it plainly indicates double speech with intent to deceive. I have known a deacon who always wanted to know his pastor's opinions about this and that, and would be quick to agree when opinions were offered. Yet he left the feeling that with another audience, he might have a contrary opinion. That is certainly a sad situation, for no man is going to be adequate for the responsibility that he is to carry in a church if he cannot be trusted to be steadfast in his convictions and responsible in his speech. The length of time that the man has been in the church is important at this point because the doubletongued man is soon discovered in his relationships to people. No such man should be made a deacon, God says.

Not given to much wine.—There is a second negative concerning the man that is to be made a deacon. He must not be given to much wine. This may seem a strange way of saying such an important thing. It is said in verse 3 that the preacher is "not given to wine." This ministerial admonition in another version is translated "temperate" and in still another version "vigilant." Many brethren have taken a great deal of comfort from the fact that while the preacher is not to use wine, the deacon is simply not to use *much* wine. They would interpret that to provide the deacon with a certain liberty in the matter of alcoholic drink, as long as it is not done, as some say, to excess. There is no real ground for believing that a double standard is created by the Scriptures. A deacon has a responsibility towards God in the matter of alcoholic drink. A fair examination of the Bible indicates that a man who is to be useful in accepting a vow that makes him a servant of the church for the rest of his life must leave intoxicating drink and even the appearance of it out of his life.

This is the place to say that abstaining from alcoholic drink is not quite enough for the deacon. He is to have nothing to do with the liquor traffic. A man that in some fashion profits from the debaucheries of men is not only a poor deacon but a poor church member. A man should not be selected as deacon in any church that in any wise is engaged in the sale of liquors. There may be a need to come back to an old-time emphasis in this matter of intoxicating drink. Perhaps the New Testament place to begin is in the office of preacher and deacon.

Dr. Paul Caudill tells of an experience in his pastorate in

Kentucky. He was asked to make a speech in the interest of banning the sale of alcoholic drinks. Activities before the election had been pretty bitter. In preparation for the speech he was to make the next day, knowing that much of his audience would be hostile, he spent a night tearing every passage out of a favorite Bible that had to do with alcoholic drink. When he was through, he had so mutilated his Bible that it was no longer of any value. A thing that is important enough to God to have such a large place in the Book is important in the life of any man that will serve God. A deacon must put out of his life any connection with, or any encouragement of, the consumption or the sale of alcoholic beverages.

Not greedy of filthy lucre.—The third thing that a deacon must not be is "greedy of filthy lucre." This is one of the most interesting things about the deacon. It is again a situation in which the preacher and the deacon are placed in contrast by a single word. Though the same English translation, "not greedy of filthy lucre," is given as a requirement for both, the words in the Greek are not the same at all. What the Bible says here certainly has been a word of caution to me as a preacher.

The preacher is not to be greedy of filthy lucre, and that has the obvious meaning that he is not to love money. It is a solemn warning against covetousness. Covetousness will ruin any Christian's life, but it will certainly ruin the ministry of a preacher. It seems to me that stealing from God by refusing to be honest about the tithe would make it impossible for a man to preach. It is not the amount of money involved that makes a man love it. Love of money is a condition of the heart, and it is against this that the solemn warning concerning the ministry is given.

The deacon, however, is not to be greedy of filthy lucre, which means literally that he is not to be "eager for base gain." The Greek word here is formed by joining two words together. The first part of the word means "base" or "dishonorable," and the last part means "gain" or "advantage." Add that together and see what the sum is. Certainly the thing that is said of the preacher is essential to the life of the deacon.

I believe the thing that makes the deacon different is that he is a person who must go out into the world and come to grips with a hard, competitive life, trying to make his living by the sweat of his brow and conscious all the while that it is a world which is built on a profit basis. Any preacher that loves his men soon finds out that that is indeed a hard grind. Some men work for salaries and feel that it is necessary to band together with others to get the proper salary and the right kind of consideration. Very likely it is; sometimes one gets only what is demanded. Others work on a commission basis, others on a fee basis, but the basic theory in all of it is that the laborer is worthy of his hire. The caution placed against the life of the deacon is that he is not to take a dishonest advantage to turn a penny of profit.

For example, it is entirely possible that a man works for another and finds that an emergency has come into the business of his employer in which he must have his services. Knowing that he is indispensable to the operation of the business, he drives as hard a bargain as he can. The question is not what is right but what he can get. On the other hand, take an employer who knows that a man cannot afford to give up his job. Perhaps the employee has a sick family or a great many financial responsibilities that make it essential for him to keep his job. Making such a man work for as little as possible is dishonest, and a man that will so do is not the right kind to make a deacon. The expression for such dishonesty that I heard used in my boyhood days was "selling material off the bottom of the pile."

Among the men that I have known—men I have loved greatly—now and again I have found one that had a disposition to drive a sharp bargain. He loved to trade; he would have made a good horse trader. In the case of a deacon, it certainly would not be right for the bargain to be too sharp or too keen. A deacon would not be a man who loved to sell a blind mule as a mule that could see. He must not be greedy of filthy lucre, that is, he must be careful about the way he makes his living.

Before going on to discuss the positive qualities that deacons should possess, it must be re-emphasized that these negative qualifications do not basically provide the kind of men out of which deacons can be made. Although there are always those things which must be left out of the life that is to count much for God, the negative qualifications for deacons should not be overemphasized. Overemphasis fits entirely too much with a conception of the deacon as a man who is solemnly removed from all the realities of life, other peoples, and bad habits, who at the same time does not count very vitally in doing the things that please God. Negativeness is not the essential quality of a deacon.

Grave.—The first positive thing that is said to Timothy by Paul concerning the deacon is that he is to be "grave." It is a word that means "venerable" or "honorable." Really, it is rather a painful word until examined very carefully. It does not describe the shape of a man's face or the length of his countenance. It is not possible to tell that a man has religion because his face is long. He may merely have bad digestion. Do not let this word destroy the plain teaching of the Scriptures that Christians are happy people and that leaders of Christians are happy in their Christian experience. The kind of men from whom God expects a New Testament church to select deacons ought to be ones that have within them a certain dignity, a consciousness of human worth and divine privilege, and a right relationship to God, making them men who can be respected, who have within them the quality of venerability.

Chapter IX points out that this word is used of deacons' wives. It is used in Titus as a requirement for the aged men. It is also used in the fourth chapter of Philippians regarding things or deeds, where it is translated "honest." The Scripture commands Christians to think about things that are grave, things of eternal significance; in other words, to have lofty thoughts. God wants his deacons to be such men, thinking such things, having such vision.

Holding the mystery of the faith in a pure conscience.— Chapter VIII discusses the things that a deacon ought to believe. He certainly should be a man of great conviction. Although the discussion of this will be reserved for that chapter, it should be borne in mind that this is one of the positive requirements for deacons.

Proved.—The next listed requirement for a deacon is that he must be proved. This is the point which needs to be presented again and again to all churches. It is so easy to be influenced by the good personality of an individual or his apparent zeal in the church that the things which have gone before in the days that he belonged to another congregation are not examined.

I was recently asked by the members of a nearby congregation to help them during a church difficulty. The church was young and had enjoyed a rather phenomenal growth. It seemed that the pastor had lost touch with the people and had assumed for himself more authority than would ever be wise. When the people had gathered and the discussion began, the chairman of the deacons was the spokesman for the dissenting group. In all fairness to him, I may say that he represented a majority opinion. As the discussion developed, it was apparent to me that the man was good but quite immature in the responsibility thrust upon him. I had opportunity to question him a bit after it was all done and discovered that he had been chairman of deacons in the church about two months and had been a member of the church about six months. In other words, he had no background of experience or Christian growth that would justify serving as a deacon much less as chairman.

It was unfortunate that a man with potentially fine promise should be so suddenly thrust into a position of responsibility for which he was not yet prepared. Having a proved, tested man in this position would have paid great dividends to the church in the time of its difficulty. I felt that the pastor who had unwisely led in the selection of leaders finally paid a price for his lack of wisdom.

The central idea of this word "proved" is that of testing or the demonstration of the individual's capacity. The same word in the New Testament is also translated "try" and "discern." In the fourteenth chapter of Luke, Jesus, talking about excuses, refers to a man who had bought five yoke of oxen and said, "I go to prove them: I pray thee have me excused." The ridiculous thing about it all was the idea that the man should have bought the oxen without first proving them. In the case of the New Testament church, it is likewise folly to put a man into a place of responsible leadership who has not been tested.

Paul exhorts the Roman Christians to prove what is the will of God. In Galatians 6:4, the instruction is to "let every man prove his own work." All of Christianity is subject to testing. Jesus invited everyone that heard him to weigh that which he said, to test it in his own heart and experience and reach a decision on that basis. If that is the principle on which the kingdom of God is built, it certainly is the principle by which God intends that men be selected for places of leadership in the churches. It corresponds to the "no novice" requirement for the preacher.

What is known about this man who is being considered? How long has he been a member of the church? What kind of service did he render in the church from which he came? What is there about his life that indicates that he is now ready to render this largest service? Questions like these are the ones that God says should be asked before selecting men for the office of deacon.

Being found blameless.—When the Scripture says that deacons should be found "blameless," it seems that a qualification has been given which any one would desire but which would necessarily elude every one. This does not say that every deacon is to be perfect, nor is such said of the preacher. A requirement of perfection would eliminate everybody, for people are not perfect. What does "blameless" mean? It means that no charge of wrongdoing has been leveled against a man or could be brought. In the qualifications set forth for the preacher, it is suggested that the man must be one against whom it is impossible to bring any charge of wrongdoing, one who can stand impartial examination. The deacon also is to be a man above reproach, one against whom no charge has been brought.

I once knew a very fine man, very prominent in Baptist life, that became involved in a number of very unpleasant political incidents. The result was that some specific charges were leveled against him that involved dishonesty. In the midst of those charges, his Baptist brethren elevated him to one of the most responsible offices that it was theirs to give. Since I believed in my friend so thoroughly, I rejoiced in the willingness to vindicate him before he had even been tried. To do this in regard to the office of deacon, however, is wrong. A man under fire—one against whom charges have been brought that relate to his life, character, or service—is not at that time ready to be chosen for the office of deacon. A man is not called to this office to protect him against such charges or give him a vote of confidence (or to reform him, for that matter). In being elevated to a responsibility that places him before the people, any man needs the best beginning that he can possibly have.

Husband of one wife, ruling his own house.—These two closing qualifications on the positive side are discussed in Chapter IX on the deacon's home. They will be considered there over against the total home background of the man that is to be a deacon.

Now what is the sum of it? The first thing is that every deacon is called to a personal examination. As the reader looks at his own life, he should weigh it against these scriptural qualifications which are set forth for the deacon as he serves in this wonderful office that has been planned of God.

Remember again that these qualities are seldom absolute. The fact that in any one of them a man may seem to fall short does not mean at all that he ought not to be a deacon. They are all capable of development. These are areas of growth in grace for the man who has been chosen of God and chosen of the church to serve as a deacon. An honest assessment may indicate strength in one and weakness in another. It is at the point of weakness that God should be asked for grace toward becoming more and better and stronger in service.

In the light of that which is found in the Scripture, there should be a church census for prospective deacons. The group in each church that is responsible for the enlistment of leaders should carefully examine the church roll, life by life. Names of the men who have proved themselves to be growing in zeal and in willingness to be all that God would have them to be should be added to the list of possibilities from

time to time. Every church has potential deacons. All has
not been done that might be done to discover them. The
purpose of this survey will be well served if it results in
bringing men who are worthy of consideration for this office
to the attention of the church.

III.

BECOMING A DEACON

O ur church business meeting in November will be the time for the election of the nominating committee," was the greeting of my deacon chairman. Since I had been pastor of the church for only two months, this had no particular significance for me. I knew that the church had a nominating committee, but it had not occurred to me to ask the manner of its election or appointment. The chairman explained that at the November meeting, nominations were received from the floor for membership on the committee. After nomination, five people were elected to this responsibility. These would prepare nominations for the active board of deacons and other elective offices of the church. Their report would be received and acted on at the December business meeting.

It seemed to me that the chairman attached unusual significance to this November meeting, but I soon thought no more of it. Church business meetings heretofore had been rather dull affairs. When this meeting came, I indicated that it was time to make nominations for the nominating committee. Five men instantly sprang to their feet. I decided which one should be recognized, and he had his nomination ready. In quick order, we had five nominations before the church. Then there was a motion that nominations cease and the five nominees be elected by acclamation. It was so plainly a matter of predetermination that I claimed the privilege of the chairman to keep the nominations open for a little while. In fact, I insisted that since we were electing five committee members, we ought to have as many as ten nominations. The next five came considerably slower. Finally nominations were done, and the election was held.

It finally became clear to me that it was an accepted practice in the church to elect those people to the nominating committee who would nominate certain preferred men as deacons. This underlined the fact that the manner in which deacons and other officers of the church are selected is very important. How can a church best carry out its responsibility of selecting men to serve as deacons?

It is presumed that the church has been instructed about what kind of men ought to fill this office. The men finally selected should be equally familiar with these requirements. In summary they are these:

1. A deacon must be willing to be all that God wants him to be.

2. He must be determined to be the very best man that he can be.

3. He must be dissatisfied with what he is.

4. He must be aware of the fact that what he can become is the result of spiritual growth, that he must grow in grace.

A man may possess all of these qualifications and yet not be selected by the church as a deacon. Certainly not all the men who are qualified are elected at the same time. Many very excellent men serve usefully in the life of the church without being selected for this office. It is important to remember that those first men in Acts, who were called the seven, were selected not for honor but for service. They were called to meet a crisis. The method of their selections is simple and clear.

A man becomes a deacon by the selection of the church. This stands in contrast to becoming a preacher. A man can become a preacher, at least in name, simply by saying he is a preacher. One announces, "God has called me to preach," and starts preaching.

I used to be pastor in a college town where there were ministerial students who were members of our congregation. The fellows were always coming to me as their pastor, wanting to be ordained. Many of them had not even been considered by churches, but they thought that somehow ordination would help their standing, open new doors, or in some way make available a ministry which otherwise would be denied. Without exception, I pointed out that a man does not have to be ordained to preach. There are street corners in town, crossroad school houses in adjacent communities, places of public gathering, multitudes of lost people, many places in which one might offer an effective preaching witness. Those who had been called to preach should get out and preach. God would open the doors.

In the matter of deacon selection, however, a man does not determine for himself that he is deacon material. He is not the one who decides that he is as capable as anyone else of serving as a deacon. It does not work that way. The New Testament pattern is that a church will make its selection of deacons at the time of need and according to the number needed. Becoming a deacon is not something to be sought, not even an ambition to be realized. It requires that an invitation be extended. It involves a service to be offered. In a large church, the selection of men to be deacons can be a very complex affair; but it is still true that the initiative must be taken by the church.

PRINCIPLES OF SELECTION

Searching the membership.—There are three principles which ought to guide a church in the selection of deacons. With faithful adherence to these principles, various methods of selection will work in the life of the church. The first principle is that the selection must be made after a careful search of the membership. Any committee or group of people charged with making nominations should search the church roll name by name. I have been present in such a meeting when a large roll was before us. The name of man after man was called aloud with a careful pause to allow us to consider his effectiveness in the church.

Congregational choice.—The second basic principle is that the selection must finally be made through democratic congregational choice. The method used for selecting deacons in the churches should be a method that gives the largest segment of the church the greatest opportunity to speak. It should be the method that opens the greatest opportunity to the church to give its best judgment in the matter. This is the general principle on which it is possible and necessary to build. Go back to the sixth chapter of Acts and find the way in which the church moved. Here, and on both sides of the passage, there was a spirit of unity and participation, with a practical address in democratic fashion to the needs of the hour and the choices to be made.

Prayerfulness.—The third principle is that these men ought to be selected by prayerful counsel with God. The democratic processes of a New Testament church are impossible without prayer. Prayer must undergird every selection, every choice, every activity of the church. If a church needs to be earnest in its praying, it should be earnest in its selection of deacons. Since the New Testament has only two offices in the church, serious, almost irreparable mistakes are made in being careless about the selection of people for these offices. It is necessary to be constantly mindful of the Holy Spirit's leadership; it is necessary to be quick in seeking his counsel and guidance.

METHODS OF SELECTION

There are many many ways in which churches select deacons. Baptists are people who manifest their independence even in processes. A discussion of some methods of selection should be helpful in evaluating the procedure of a church.

Nomination by deacons.—One of the first methods with which I became acquainted was the nomination of new deacons by the old ones. In a particular church where I served, the deacons often would get the feeling that a few more deacons were needed. They would discuss it awhile and perhaps carry over from meeting to meeting. Finally, nominations would be made to the church. It was tacitly understood that any nominations that were to be made should come from the deacon group itself. There is no question in my mind about the wisdom, the prayerfulness, and the ability of the deacons in Baptist churches. However, this method manifested some serious disadvantages.

In the first place, it was not done at regular intervals. The matter usually came up for consideration when some man had made his presence felt in the church a little more than most of the others. Then the question arose as to whether or not he should be a deacon.

There is a great question as to the wisdom of the nominations for successors coming from a group which has, in effect, the power to establish and operate a closed corporation. A group of deacons then becomes a self-perpetuating body. Self-perpetuating bodies in Baptist life are not according to the New Testament pattern. There is a tendency for such bodies to be short in the matters of spirit and accomplishment, and long in a sense of being indispensable and in a failure to recognize the worth of the total fellowship.

All of the churches that use this method do not choose unwisely. Undoubtedly there are few people in the church who could choose better, more effective men than could those who occupy the office of deacon. In churches where fellowship is fine, this method has often been used with a good degree of success. I simply suggest that because of its departure from the normal pattern of Baptist life, it is not the best method for making such selection.

Nomination by the pastor.—Another method, not in such common use but practiced by some churches, is the nomination of deacons by the pastor. Let me hasten to say that I think that no man ought to be nominated as a deacon without consulting the pastor. If there is one man in the church that is vitally interested in this selection, it is the pastor. The position to which God has called him and the confidence of the people that his leadership in the church is a work of the Holy Spirit make it necessary to consider his judgment. He is the man in whom all the church should have utmost confidence. His people regard him as a man of God, a man led of the Holy Spirit. They believe that their relationship with him is born of the will of God. This is all fine, and it makes the pastor vitally concerned with the selection of deacons.

Yet as has been said concerning the first method, this second method lacks much. Measure it against the principles with which the discussion was begun. A Baptist church means congregational church government, yet we Baptists are not always as careful as we should be to let the congregation make decisions. I once had a deacon friend tell me that he thought the reason he was made a deacon was that the pastor at the time was a close friend. They played dominoes together. He felt that perhaps their friendship had something to do with the pastor's recommendation. I feel sure that that must have been an overstatement of it, but there is a tendency for one-man nominations to be colored by personal friendships.

Notice that in the first selection the word used is "appointed." The verses that surround this passage, however, indicate that the men were not directly appointed by the apostles but elected by the congregation. The word itself is translated elsewhere as "ordain," "make ruler," "set," and "conduct." Selection by the pastor is not the healthiest method for a church, considering its future welfare. Consult the pastor by all means. Take a long time before making a man a deacon who could not have the approval of his pastor, but remember always that the church itself must speak.

The nominating committee.—The third method for the selection and presentation of men to the church as possible deacons is the use of a nominating committee. This may be either a special committee selected for the occasion or a standing nominating committee (the procedure of many churches). A special committee appointed for the occasion should be representative of the whole church. It should take the character of the office into consideration and should be composed of people who have some knowledge of the New Testament requirements for deacons. It would be good to have both men and women on the committee. Whether a special or standing committee is used, the method of its selection will be determined by church action.

The manner in which a standing nominating committee is to be chosen is a matter of immediate importance. There are churches like the one mentioned at the beginning of the chapter which choose such a committee by nomination from the floor. A rather safe principle in so selecting a committee is to nominate at least twice as many people as are needed to serve. This provides for a democratic selection by the church. The committee may be appointed by the pastor, if that is the custom of the church. It may be selected by the retiring nominating committee as all the other church committees are selected and presented to the church for election. Whatever the method of securing this nominating committee, the church should feel that it is its own committee and that all the people of the church will be considered in its work.

There is an added word in favor of this standing nominating committee in considering the work it does. A standing committee considers personnel and offices in the church all year long. Not only does it present nominations for deacons but also names of men and women to serve as other officers of the church and its organizations. This means that the committee will have a real knowledge of the membership of the church, and will take every precaution to choose wisely in order that it can recommend with a conviction that its choices are the will of God.

Deacons nominated directly by the congregation.—As a fourth method, it is entirely proper that deacons may be nominated from the floor. This allows the initiative to be taken by the congregation. This purpose may also be achieved by having members of the congregation write on a ballot the names of men whom they think should be considered. To say that these methods are risky simply means that they risk embarrassment to the person making the nomination or the person nominated. In following this method, it becomes necessary that if a person is nominated who is not qualified in the light of the New Testament, someone must openly say so. If the church decides that it wants the frank, openly democratic method of public consideration, then it must be just as frank, loving, spiritual, and honest in openly evaluating the person who has been nominated.

General observations on method.—There are some things which should be mentioned concerning method. No method by its nature will guard against error. There is no mechanical device which guarantees that the men who are selected are the men who should have been selected. This limitation of method can be seen in church bylaws. Occasionally a church searches for a set of bylaws by which it can restore harmony. It never works. The problems of harmony and of working together are spiritual. So it is in nominating the men from whom the church will select deacons. A church that is prayerful, spiritual, alert, and responsive to the will of God can use any one of many methods and make it work. However, a church will want to make a wise selection of method.

A wise procedure is to nominate at least twice as many men as are to be elected. When a successor for Judas was chosen, two were nominated, but one was elected. If the early church found this a proper approach to democracy, Baptists today could well use it. Someone may object that the method is embarrassing for the man who is nominated but not elected. It should not be. No man could be more highly honored by a New Testament church than to have his name placed on a list of nominations for deacons. Many who have served the church faithfully are not considered. In fact, the nomination itself will place an added responsibility on a man's life.

Using the deacon list.—Should the churches which practice the rotation of deacons (discussed in Chapter IV) give special consideration to men who have been ordained as deacons whether in this church or another, but are not actively serving at the time? It would be good to give them consideration based not upon their previous ordination but upon their own present service in the church. The fact that a man has been previously ordained does not entitle him to honor without service.

In our church, the names of all men who have been previously ordained are placed on a list. The nominating committee also selects two names for each vacancy, and these two lists are put together. This new list is used as a nominating ballot. By vote on this ballot, the church nominates twice as many men as are to be elected. At a later meeting, final election is made from this nominated group. This is a cumbersome method but serves as part of a democratic process which is workable as an application of basic New Testament principles.

"These are our deacons," must be the sentiment that follows the election. It is not good in a Baptist church to hear members of the congregation refer to "those deacons," which reflects a common attitude when someone else has selected the deacons. God has ordained the office of deacon, and the selection of those who fill it is a responsibility given by God to the members of the congregation. A sense of possession on the part of the congregation will mean a promise of prayer, encouragement, and support for the service which the men are to render the church.

When to elect.—The time of the election is not a matter of primary importance to be sure. Occasionally, someone says that deacons ought to be elected at one of the regular Sunday services, in spite of the fact that all the other business of the church is transacted on Wednesday night at a regular business meeting. It is a matter that is important enough for consideration at any time. It is no more important than any other command of God or any other program given to the churches of God. The recommendation is that it be made a part of the regular business procedure of the church. Notice will be given if the church is not accustomed to the time, and church publications will carry any necessary information. The congregation will be encouraged to be present, but a regular business meeting time will serve the best objectives in the long run.

PERSONAL COMMITTAL

The nature of the deacon's office demands more than nomination and election by a church. It is not simply an office to be gained or a distinction to be achieved; it is a service to be rendered and a life to be dedicated. This always must be a two-way transaction. A man may be chosen by the church to be a deacon and occupy the office in a mechanical sense without being a New Testament deacon in the true spiritual sense. He may not have committed himself at all to the function which God has put within his reach. An example is found in the matter of baptism. A man who is not a Christian can be immersed, but he cannot be baptized in the real New Testament spiritual sense. New Testament baptism is believer's baptism and marks a committal previously made in the heart to Jesus. It is equally true that a man may be set apart as a deacon who is not one in real truth.

To a relationship.—First of all, serving as a deacon is a committal to a relationship. A man is not made a deacon to honor him. It is an honor beyond most of the things that can come to a man's life, but that is not the primary consideration. The deacon is set apart to serve. It is to that service and to the relationship which it involves, that a man must commit his life. The new deacon should understand that he has not been elected to an official board to exercise authority in the life of the church. The New Testament office of deacon is not an office of authority but of service. By accepting this service in his life, he actually forfeits some personal privileges to be individualistic. No man can be an effective deacon who has not recognized that he is giving up much privilege in favor of service.

The term which describes his dedicated life is "servant." It is this position of first servant which places a man on the spot before his church. What does the deacon serve? He serves a New Testament church of which Christ is the head. When the church makes expression of its will, it remains for a dedicated man to carry out that will, whatever it may cost personally. The only possible exception to this would be when the will expressed by the church is immoral or dishonest, and that is a very farfetched concept.

There must be a time when deacons soberly consider the implications of the place and personally dedicate themselves to the opportunity which is God given. No man has a right to turn away from such a dedication except for a reason that God would approve. It cannot be emphasized enough that there is no more serious, sober choice in life than to give one's self to the service of Christ and to the will of his church, for all of life.

To an exampleship.—Such a committal carries with it a secondary responsibility of exampleship which is just as binding as the first. The man who agrees to serve as a deacon in a New Testament church agrees to be an example, to the limit of God's enduement, in all the life of the church. He is to be an example in spirit, love, devotion, and loyalty. A deacon should be as loyal in the program of the church as the preacher is. He should be an example in every realm.

This certainly means an example in attendance. How would it be if the membership of the church attended Training Union like the deacons? Examples, to be effective, need to be seen. There are other areas such as stewardship and soul-winning where the deacon will commit himself to exampleship.

THE ORDINATION

When the church has made its selection of deacons and these men have committed themselves to the office in all its meaning of service, there remains in our Baptist churches the service of ordination. The New Testament speaks of a "laying on of hands." Dr. Dobbins has said that this was "a beautiful ceremonial service of recognition of fitness, approval of selection, and expression of benediction." [1] There are certain principles that ought to govern the service of ordination.

[1] Gaines S. Dobbins, *The Churchbook.* Nashville: The Broadman Press, 1951, p. 69.

First, it should be at a time that magnifies the office. As nearly as possible, the membership of the church ought to be present. Much publicity should be given to the fact that there is to be an ordination service. It should be conducted with dignity and sincerity as a sacred moment in the life of the church as well as in the life of the man. Every ordination service should have a moment of explanation of the office of deacon. Too much cannot be said to the church about what the office signifies and the service which this man to be ordained has accepted. The ordination prayer should be led by someone selected by the pastor and approved by the men to be ordained.

There follows the laying on of hands, which is the most directly scriptural part of the procedure. This is not the actual bestowing of a mantle, even spiritually. We who have been ordained have no spiritual power that can be automatically transferred from one man to another by the physical act of a hand laid upon his head. It is a promise of prayer and encouragement, an acceptance into a wonderful fellowship, and a recognition of a divine institution. Following the laying on of hands, it is good for the church to extend the hand of fellowship to the newly ordained men. Much would be lost by getting away from the hand extended in Christian greeting and fellowship.

As a pastor, I have been to a great many ordination services and have always found a blessing in the presence of the dedication of life which is involved. After the service, greetings are exchanged on every side, and there is a moment of happy fellowship in the life of the church. Soon the people will be turning away from the service, with the new deacons having been ordained. What is to be the future of this moment? What is the next thing that takes place? All too often this is not simply the end of the chapter but of the book. That is not as it should be, for a foundation has been laid for a life that can transform a church and make its contribution to God's great program of redemption. A new world has opened, and a new day has dawned, in the life of a dedicated man.

IV

HOW MANY AND HOW LONG?

THE NUMBER OF DEACONS

In my church," said one pastor, "we follow the Scriptures. We have seven deacons, just the number that the Book says. I believe that if that was adequate for the church at Jerusalem, it is good enough for my church. In fact, I have discovered that with only seven deacons, I do not need to have deacons' meetings. I can call them together when I want them, and I don't have to be worried about strife between the preacher and a 'board' of deacons."

"I would rather not have deacons in my church than to have only seven," said another pastor. "In our church we have, I suppose, seventy-five deacons. I have found that you need a large number of deacons in order to have a reasonable representation at your meeting. If we are to have enough to do the things that our deacons really can do in the church, the number must be so great that the working group will be large enough to do it."

"It seems to me that you are pretty far apart," I said. "Seven seems such a few in a church of several hundred members. At the same time, I would hate to concede in the very beginning that half of my deacons were not going to attend and were not going to serve. I believe that these would corrupt the other half. I would rather have a selected group of deacons that have agreed to work. I want the number itself to indicate to the men that they are expected to be faithful and are needed in the performance of the task."

These three viewpoints do not represent all of the situations that exist in Baptist churches. Churches of the same size have vastly different numbers of deacons.

There would be many answers to the question directed to a pastor, "What determined the number of deacons in your church?" A pastor friend said to me recently, "The rule which I follow in recommending the number of deacons for our church is one to each one hundred members. I have found that that ratio establishes a good working basis for getting the things done that are necessary." At least, he was seeking to establish a sensible rather than a sentimental basis for the number of deacons in the church.

The seven.—The first chapter of this book insisted that we have the office of deacon because it is a New Testament institution. It was set up in the wisdom of God in the earliest days of the New Testament church. Accepting that as a first premise, it certainly becomes necessary to follow the Scriptures in every possible detail regarding the office. If my pastor friend was right that the Scriptures intend to set up a standard number, then all would want to follow it. The question is whether Luke's history established seven as the proper number of deacons in a church. It is worth careful review.

Remember that the men in the sixth chapter of Acts were not called deacons. The work "service" is used in the chapter, but there is no clear evidence that a definite office was established. Philip was described in the twenty-first chapter of Acts as "one of the seven." This was the commonly-accepted title for these first men. It remained for succeeding generations to describe them as deacons in terms of an office. Of course, Luke may have regarded this as the institution of the office which established a new departure rather than merely an isolated incident. Such an emphasis is characteristic of a historian who was fond of recording the beginnings of movements.

It was not long until the question of number was brought up in those first churches. An early church tradition speaks of Stephen and Nichol..s as ordained to the deaconate. The same writer speaks of Stephen as the first deacon. For centuries, the Roman church continued to restrict the number to seven. A canon enacted by one of the councils of Caesarea (A.D. 314) stated that "there ought to be but seven deacons in any city." St. Mark is said to have ordained seven deacons at Alexandria. What was the explanation given in these various situations for the fact that there were only seven?

The answers are many and, of course, speculative. Some say that the number seven was fixed upon because of the seven traditional gifts of the Spirit. Others say that the number was fixed with regard to the different elements of the church. These suggest that there were three parts Hellenist, three parts Hebrew, and one part proselyte. That certainly could not be determined with any accuracy. Someone else, thinking no doubt of our modern cities divided into their various sections, suggests that Jerusalem may have been divided into seven districts and that a deacon presided over each district. One writer says that there were seven distinct congregations in Jerusalem. The number of the disciples at that particular time was certainly large enough to have justified such a division.

It might be more plausible to agree with those who say that the number was determined from a consideration of the sacred quality attached to the number seven by the Jews. Seven was the sacred number, the number of completeness. In Revelation, for example, "seven" occurs about fifty times and is applied to a great variety of persons and things. All through the Scriptures this number is to be found. Our Lord's choice of twelve disciples was the practical use of a number sacred in its associations for every Israelite. From this, it is argued that the number seven may have been adopted because of its sacredness in Jewish eyes. Thus side by side with the twelve apostles, a group which came to its end with the death of the apostles, there existed at this period another group, the seven deacons. Most of these suggestions contain an element of demonstrated proof and, perhaps, a larger element of speculation.

There is nothing in Scripture to suggest that the number was actually a matter of vital importance. It is hard to believe that the Holy Spirit would have omitted any word regarding the number in setting up the qualifications for the office in Paul's first letter to Timothy, if this was to be scripturally determined. The emphasis in the sixth chapter of Acts is not on the number but on the task to which the men were called and the relationship which they represented in the church. The Scriptures do not, therefore, fix the number seven as one that every church ought to adopt. Some smaller churches would have great difficulty in finding seven men who would meet the demands of the office and give themselves to its service.

Principles that govern the number.—The deacons of the New Testament churches had to do with the membership. Theirs was no impersonal office. In the first task that was assigned them, they had to deal directly with people. It seems to follow inevitably that the number of deacons in the church must have something to do with the number of members that are to be served. There is no reason to believe that there should be as many deacons in the church of a hundred members as in one of a thousand members. Whatever the ratio to be followed, the size of the membership certainly should have a bearing upon the number of deacons finally decided upon.

My friend's ratio of one deacon to a hundred members would mean about fifty families to a deacon in an average church. A serious program of work in which the deacon actually serves the families for which he is made responsible would make that ratio a little large. The resident church membership will be the determining factor in this matter. This should be divided into practical working units, and the number of deacons should be sufficient to serve the people.

One of the basic principles is that the office of deacon is to be an office of service rather than primarily an office of honor. However many men are chosen by a church, it should be a group that actually works and serves. Perhaps the number whom the church wishes to honor would be large. The deaconate is not for that purpose. A man who is a deacon is expected to serve. The demands of service, as determined by the size of the church, should control the number of deacons.

It is entirely possible that the number of deacons in a church will be limited by the number of qualified men who are available. Men ought not to be elected and set apart to the office of deacon simply because a certain number is needed. Unqualified men do not have to be accepted. It would be better for the church to do its work with fewer men than actually needed, than to select the wrong men for the office. Of course, such a condition does not have to be accepted as permanent. The search should go on constantly for men who do qualify and are willing to serve. A preparation period in the lives of some men, involving careful instruction as to the meaning of the office, might supply the need for more deacons.

THE TERM OF OFFICE

Lifetime service.—"Once a deacon, always a deacon," is an ancient Baptist precept. When a man has been selected and ordained by a Baptist church to serve as deacon, it is generally accepted that he is a Baptist deacon as long as he lives. The only limitation of this has been that a man's ordination may be revoked for wrong conduct. The references to Philip in the Scripture cover a longer span of years than those to any of the other seven; and in the last reference, he is still identified as one of the seven. The instances are very few in Baptist life where a deacon is ever put aside from office.

In a church that I used to serve, there was a young man who had been made a deacon prior to my connection with the church. There came a period of unrest, and my predecessor as pastor had great difficulty with many of the members. This young man, though one of the deacons, allied himself with the group opposed to the pastor. When the hour of crisis finally came, the pastor mustered enough support to have this man put out of office because he had manifested positive antagonism to the pastor's leadership. I believe that the pastor was right in leading the church to "dedeac" him. Finally, however, the pastor was forced to leave the church; and the first action of the church was to "redeac" this same man. The scars were evident in the life of this deacon all through my relationship to the church.

On the other side, some of the sweetest chapters in the lives of Baptist churches are those that revolve around the lives of men who have served the church over a long, long period as deacon. I could never cease to be grateful to God for one man who had served as chairman of the deacons for more than thirty years in a church to which I was called. Sweet of spirit, faithful of heart, wise in his choices, the vision of youth still his, he blessed the life of a young preacher beyond describing. Many of us think with gratitude of the heritage of the home of this father and husband who served his church as deacon for more than half a century.

Should there be definite terms of office in which men serve actively as deacons? This is not a question as to whether men of real Christian stature will serve the church at all times. There are some men who will remain towers of strength in the church whether they are called active or inactive deacons. Regardless of this fact, many churches have discovered that by having an active group of deacons serving for a definite period of time, they have been able to train more men and use them more effectively in the whole church program. Many of the difficulties that have grown up around the office (and in some places have brought it into disrepute) have been eliminated by instituting a system of rotation, a definite tenure of office which may be repeated again and again in the life of a single deacon. In the absence of any scriptural instruction at this point, the practical, demonstrated values of the plan should be the guide.

Definition of rotation.—What does rotation of deacons mean? It means that a man is asked to serve with a group of active deacons for a period of, say, three years. At the end of that time, his term is concluded, and he continues to serve only if re-elected by the church. In one church that I served, there were forty active deacons. Each deacon served for a four-year term. Ten of the forty terms would expire each year. Thus ten places had to be filled by the church each year. In another pastorate, the number of deacons was thirty-six. The term in this church was three years, with twelve vacancies to be filled annually. Rotation is now in very general use in Southern Baptist churches.

Starting rotation.—Churches that do not use the rotation plan follow various methods in selecting men to serve as deacons. In some, all the men who have been ordained are recognized as active deacons, including the ordained man who comes from another church. Such a group may be large and unwieldy, but there is usually a smaller working unit within the group. There are other churches that recognize all of the men that have been ordained by the particular church but do not recognize ordained men coming from another church. In either case, the place to begin in setting up a rotation system is the discussion of the system as a practical way of using more men and obtaining each man's largest contribution to the life of the church. I believe that no church should enter the practice of rotation until it has been adequately considered by all, and both pastor and deacons have agreed that it is an opportunity for improvement. Once this point of agreement has been reached, there are some problems, more apparent than real, that must be solved.

The number of deacons needed in active service will have to be determined. The principles for this have already been discussed, and the decision should be easily made. A more serious question concerns the men who have served as deacons over a long period and feel that being placed on an inactive roll for even a year would mean placing them on the shelf. These are good men. They are not necessarily self-seeking or ambitious. They feel that they have a contribution to make which will be cut off if they are put aside for even a brief period. It goes without saying that every effort should be made to avoid any damage to the life of any one of these. Men that have served faithfully through the years are worthy of the greatest consideration when such a change is anticipated.

If this problem arises, one effective answer is to be found in a consideration of the number of years that such men have served. Suppose there are three men that have served as active deacons for twenty years each. In the establishment of a new system, they could be made life members, with the understanding that life tenure would not be the practice after that time. Inserting the principle into a new system of making all men that have served twenty years eligible for life membership would not be good. Life membership is a way, however, to provide at the beginning of rotation for the man who has served long, without allowing him to feel that he is now being pushed aside. Perhaps the matter does not deserve this much discussion. In many churches, these men will be the first to say that rotation is a necessity. Its values are so obvious that they are the first to volunteer to accept a year of retirement to let others have the privilege of service.

Once these questions have been resolved, the actual institution of the system is very easy. The plan of nomination will have to be determined. Whether committee or open nomination is adopted, every ordained man in the church ought to receive consideration as well as those new men whose service, faithfulness, character, and potentialities stamp them as ones to whom consideration should be given. For the first election, it should be agreed that terms will be staggered so that an equal number will retire each year. Thus a set number of vacancies will occur each year after this, each to be filled for a full term. If a three-year system has been decided on, perhaps the fairest way is to let those receiving the greatest number of votes be three-year men, the second group two-year men, and the last group one-year men. In a four year system, the division could be made equitably in the same fashion.

One year off.— It has been found that the rotation system works most successfully and brings the greatest advantage to the church when it is agreed that a man may not be considered for re-election at the conclusion of his term until one year has elapsed. I once was pastor of a church which had a three-year term for active service. The trouble was that there was no required interval between the conclusion of one term and the beginning of another. Hence there was a practical succession in office that did away with actual rotation. Men automatically succeeded themselves, and there was a great deal of hesitancy to suggest anyone for consideration over against those who were serving. The one-year interval is a "must" if a church is to benefit by the rotation plan.

Its advantages are obvious. By providing an opportunity to use a new group of men in the office of deacon, it is really an open door for new blood, which is always good. It thus increases the number of men in the church who are in active touch with its life as deacons.

This period also provides an answer to an embarrassing situation that sometimes arises. Here is a man who has been serving on the active group of deacons but whose service has been altogether inadequate. It may be that he simply does not "deac." After he has been off the active group for a year, it is very easy for the church to make a change without any personal embarrassment. If he is eligible to succeed himself immediately, not being re-elected is a personal affront.

A third advantage is that the year that a deacon is not on the active group provides a real testing of his actual worthiness for the office. Such remarks as these are not uncommon: "I am sure looking forward to my year's rest. Just three more months now, and I can fish all I want to." Or, "It's not my problem any more; you fellows will just have to tend to it. I sure am relieved." Again, "Well, I served my term." All such remarks indicate that the deacon feels that he can now spend a year at ease in the life of the church. Not so. This year will be one of the most vital in all his service of the church. He is still a deacon. He is a marked man by reason of his vow in this particular position as a servant of the church. Actually, he is to have an opportunity to do some things in the church that usually is not his. There are tasks that are not assigned to the active group of deacons. The zeal that he manifests, the soul-winning that he does, the interest that he takes in the whole program, and the faithfulness with which he participates are all measuring sticks by which the church may know that this man is indeed worthy of every honor and every opportunity for service.

The deacon from another church.—A question that is related to the matter of term of office is that one which concerns deacons who move from one church to another. Should they be immediately recognized as deacons and received into the active group of deacons in the new church? In one church that I served such men were accepted, and they became a part of the active deacon group. In still another pastorate, they were recognized as deacons, and their ordination was accepted. Instead of being received into the active group of deacons, however, they were simply regarded as material from which other deacons might be selected. There should be no question about recognition of these men as ordained deacons. Any church in granting the letter for a deacon should indicate his being a deacon in the letter. Ordination will be recognized by the new church, and the man will be in truth one of the deacons of the church even though not serving in the active group.

As an illustration, take the case of the preacher who becomes a member of a church of which he is not pastor. It has been my privilege to be pastor of several churches with other ministers as members. These men were ordained ministers and were so regarded in the church. In the annual letter to the association, they were listed as ordained preachers who were members of the church, but they were not pastors of the church. (They might even be pastors of churches which they serve elsewhere.) The point is that being an ordained Baptist preacher does not make it necessary that a man is also pastor of the church to which he belongs. It is equally true that a deacon ordained by a Baptist church has a lifelong separation mark placed upon him. When he transfers to another church, he is still an ordained deacon. Unless character or conduct make it necessary to change his status, he remains such for all his life in any church where he goes. It does not, however, necessarily follow that he is a member of the active group of deacons in the particular church to which he goes. In fact, it is far better and he is far more honored in being sought out by the definite selection of the new church than in coming automatically into office by reason of his transfer of letter.

In line with the qualifications for a deacon that are laid down in the Scripture, a man ought to be tested. This means that he is tested not only in the church which ordained him but equally in the church to which he goes after he is ordained. There is too much at stake for a church suddenly to lay hands on a man—or, more exactly, to lay office on a man —who has not had the opportunity to prove himself. When this is thus explained, no right-thinking man would desire early induction into office in the particular church to which he has moved his membership.

Recognize all deacons.—There are some things which a church should do to keep itself deacon conscious and to keep the deacon fresh in the recognition of the vow of service which is his. A roll of all the ordained deacons in the church should be maintained. This roll should be published from time to time in order that the entire membership of the church may be well acquainted with it. Whether a particular man is serving on the active group or not, it should be established in the minds of the members that he is an ordained deacon. He is not to attend the regular monthly meetings of the deacons, but he is to be recognized in the church as an ordained deacon.

Every effort should be made to see that these men who are ordained are given great opportunities to serve in the life and program of the church. When workers are needed, the church should first make reference to this deacon roll. What each man is doing in the church should be considered. The most capable, the most interested, and the most willing group of any in the church should be found here.

An annual recognition of some kind would certainly be in order for this group. This could bring all the group together for one special service when the office of deacon, with its many privileges and opportunities, would be renewed in the life of the church. The church bulletin used that morning might contain the names of all these men. Another kind of recognition could be a social event that brings all of the deacons together. Whatever the medium used, it is worthwhile for the church during each year to call attention to the fact that these men are ordained and that they are responsible to God and their church for a particular type of service and manner of life.

In one of my pastorates, there was a man who had been a deacon a long time. He was zealous, faithful, and consecrated. Although a little quick spoken and quite frank in what he said, he was warm of heart. He had proved his value to the church in many, many ways. The time came when the church decided to adopt the rotation plan and this deacon was elected to the first group that was to serve. When his term was up, he entered his year of enforced absence from the active group with all the grace in the world. It was during this period that I came to be his pastor. He was so warm in his support of the new pastor, so encouraging in his attitudes and young in his vision, that I was quite certain that when the time came for the election of deacons, he would be returned to the active group. He was not elected but was the man next in line in the number of votes received. I grieved about it personally, but he himself was happy that some younger men had been chosen to serve. He was as faithful and as ready in his service as any man who was elected that year. When it came time for election the next year, he was elected. What a tribute to a man's spirit and faithfulness that even though he was a little advanced in years, his service was recognized as a thing needed by the church. This man showed the attitude that deacons need, whether they are serving with the active group or not. It is this attitude of service which qualifies a man for a place in the active deacon group.

It would be good to make one's own list of advantages that are found in a rotation system. By way of summary, there are four that I would like to suggest. In the first place, the plan uses and develops more men. Development is impossible except through activity. The plan also prevents intrusion of personalities into the selection of personnel of the deacon group. Then, the plan underlines the fact that the men are there not for honor but for work. They are not serving as a board of directors but as a vital group of servants in the life of a New Testament church. Finally, the plan opens the door to younger men, thereby enlarging the opportunity for Christian service in the church.

V.

THE DEACON AND THE CHURCH MEMBERSHIP

Y ou have been chosen chairman of our deacons," I said to my friend as he sat across from me in my office. "I want you to know that that is entirely in accord with my wishes. When asked by the nominating committee if I had preferences as to chairman, I answered that any member of the group could serve as chairman with my full approval and encouragement. Now, I feel that it is only fair to you to tell you what is involved. You know that I count upon my deacons for a program of hard work. They mean more to me as pastor than they can possibly know. I will feel perfectly free to call upon you as chairman by day or by night, even in the midnight hour without apology. I will feel no hesitancy in asking you to lead our group to do anything that needs to be done for the good of the church and the extension of its program. I will make demands upon your time that will seem almost impossible. I believe from my heart that you are willing to pay the price and that the men who serve as deacons in this church are willing to pay the price in hard work."

"You can count on me," he said earnestly. "I believe that I am as busy as most men in our group, but I am certainly determined to make my deacon responsibility a primary responsibility."

I wish that I had kept books on how much time this man actually spent at his job. Not only did he spend time at it, but under his progressive leadership, all of the group discovered afresh that this matter of being a deacon is a thing that

involves hard work. Much time, primary loyalties, and all
the rest convince me that in the hearts of most men who
have accepted the honor of the deacon's place and have
yielded themselves to its responsibility, there is a real willingness to serve and to work. All too many of our churches
simply have not opened to them opportunities for service,
and the things which a deacon ought to do are not made
clear. Many could raise the question of my Virginia friend,
"What ought my husband to do as a deacon?"

There is certainly no more fundamental question than the
one that concerns the actual work of the deacon. Anyone
who is given a job would like to know what the job is and
what it entails. The first answer is that a deacon is to *do*
something. He is elected to a program of hard work. Looking pious or being prominent will not suffice. The first group
of seven went to work. Whatever else they did, the phrase
"to serve tables" indicates that they were immediately assigned to a definite responsibility. Do deacons know exactly
what they are supposed to do? Here are some of the areas
for service.

The first major premise in a deacon's work is this: *There
are no duties in the Scriptures specifically and exclusively
assigned to the deacon.* Repeat that phrase over and over,
and then search the Scriptures to prove its truth. The seven
men of Acts 6 looked after the needy in that first church;
but after the Jerusalem conference, the one caution still laid
upon the preachers in their ministry to the Gentiles was that
they should not neglect the widows and the poor. Others
certainly share in this benevolence responsibility with the
deacons in most churches. There are things which church
custom and tradition assign to the deacons, but these are not
scripturally assigned. Deacons are really expected to do anything that the church desires of them.

The New Testament deacon had a work to do with refer-

ence to the membership of the church. The original seven
men were in fact concerned with personal relations in the
church. In freeing the apostles, who can be compared to
pastors, to their major work of prayer and preaching, the
deacons had to accept pastoral functions. Making distribution to the needs of the widows in the church was something
which had previously been a part of the apostles' pastoral
ministry. Undoubtedly, the apostles felt keenly the needs of
every one of the members. These deacons were to feel the
needs of the membership just as keenly and were to address
themselves to such needs in a fashion that pleased the
church.

To secure the better fellowship in the church which the
deacon office was designed to provide, the man who fills the
office must do many things with reference to the membership that will make such harmony and fellowship possible.
There are no men in the church about whom the members
know more than they know about the deacons who serve
them. It is also true that there are no men in the church that
know more about the members than the men selected by the
church to serve as deacons. Therefore, one of the chief areas
of service for deacons is to be found in their work as it relates to the congregation.

THE DEACON AND THE DEACONS

One of the first things a deacon can do is to recognize a
particular responsibility, that which exists in his relationship
to his fellow deacons. This is an unusual group of men to
which the deacon belongs. Deacons are unusual in their abilities, or they would not have been selected. They are unusual in their church attitudes and faithfulness. There is a
tie that binds them together in the acceptance of the office
that makes for an unusual relationship. Each deacon should
be very conscious of the fact that he is responsible to this
group for doing certain definite things.

Attendance of deacons' meetings.—Belonging to a group brings responsibility for attendance upon the meetings of the group. This is surely true of deacons. Such attendance is not always easy. I have known some deacons who were travelling men. In spite of the fact that their jobs required that they be away from their homes each week, they made their plans and engagements far enough in advance that when deacons' meeting night came, their presence could be expected. If a man cannot attend the meetings of the deacons, he should not be elected to a place of service on the active group.

A church should help to make it possible for the deacons to be faithful in their attendance. Meetings of the group should be planned a year in advance and placed on the church calendar. The convenient time for the meeting will vary with different churches. Some will meet on Sunday afternoon, although this time certainly has its drawbacks. As busy as Sundays usually are, it is a little difficult to take the afternoon for still another meeting. In my church, we meet on Monday night after the first Sunday. The point is that the time of the meeting should be determined by the church well in advance and the men given an opportunity to make definite plans for the meeting.

The time ought to be protected in the activities of the church. I would not say that a meeting date should never be changed. It ought to be changed, however, only for very good reasons acceptable to, and agreed upon by, the whole group. A revival meeting date sometimes has to conflict with a set time, particularly where the revival involves co-operative or simultaneous evangelism with the other churches. In such a case, the deacons would surely want to change. Repeated changes, however, will often defeat the best intentions of the men to be faithful in their attendance. Incidental competition in the church program with the deacons meeting time is inexcusable.

The program of the deacons' meeting should be carefully planned. This is not simply to make the meeting attractive to the deacon who attends it, though that certainly is a justifiable consideration. Such planning is in order that the busy people who make up the group may have the privilege of scheduling other engagements and still include the deacons' meeting. It becomes the chairman's responsibility to see that the meeting begins on time, that an agenda has been carefully prepared, and that it is carefully followed. These meetings are primarily for reports and for planning further activities. Usually an hour is sufficient for the regular deacons' meeting. Some actual deacons' meetings, of course, do not compare too well with this standard.

Actually in our church, we have about three different meetings of the deacons on the regular meeting night. The first takes place for about twenty minutes prior to the meeting when the men begin to meet each other at the door as they come in for the session. It is amazing how glad they are to see each other and how many things they have to talk about. Very gradually they move towards the place of meeting and the chairman finally calls the meeting to order. Then there is the regular meeting which I have been discussing.

The third meeting begins as soon as the prayer of adjournment is finished. The deacons visit for a little while in the room, then some of them drift out into the hall with little discussion groups to be found up and down the hall of the church. On a pleasant evening, the meeting finally moves out onto the sidewalk, where men will stand on the corner and talk with each other just as though they had not seen each other the day before. It is really a very wonderful thing that the right kind of deacons' meeting becomes in the life of a church.

Make it as easy as possible for the deacons to attend the meeting. The deacons, on the other hand, will make every effort possible to be present. Social excuses would not be considered valid along side the importance of the regular meeting of this group. Attendance is a "must" if a deacon is to serve faithfully in his office.

Serving officially.—Another responsibility which the deacon ought to accept in his deacon fellowship is the responsibility of doing whatever he is asked to do in the organization of the group. Does the group want to elect him as their chairman? If so, there is but one answer that the right kind of a deacon can give. Hesitation at this point by a man who has had experience serving as a deacon would be readily understood. Being chairman of the deacons is a hard job and involves much real work. A church has a way of looking upon the chairman of the deacons as an official receiver of all complaints. If there is something the people do not like, they talk to the chairman of the deacons. If there is a program that they want initiated, they feel that this man is particularly suited to start the program.

Consider a few things that the good chairman will do. He is in every sense a right-hand man to the pastor. He will be worthy of the pastor's confidence and respect. He should be a constant source of encouragement. In the absence of the pastor, he will see to it that no unusual crisis disturbs the fellowship of the church. In cases of sudden illness on the part of the pastor, the chairman steps in to see that a pulpit committee functions and that the full program of the church is carried on.

He is to preside at every deacons' meeting. In a personal way, the chairman will feel a responsibility for the attendance of the deacons. I have always considered it a good thing for the chairman of the deacons to have available for his own consideration an attendance record of the members of the deacon group upon the worship services of the church. If a problem of conduct arises upon the part of some member of the group, the chairman should be the first to sit down with him as a brother and try to help him see his responsibility. By virtue of his office, the chairman becomes a man that feels the responsibility of the church's program and witness, a little more keenly than anyone else except the pastor.

Because of the number of responsibilities that come to the chairman, it is well for him to serve for a limited time only. In the first place, the time that is required should not be constantly demanded of one person. This very heavy responsibility should be passed around to the other men. In the second place, it is the sort of responsibility that should be made available to as many men as possible. In the course of church service, responsibilities such as this provide a great opportunity for growth.

Again and again through the years, I have had a nominating committee from the deacons come to me as pastor and say, "Pastor, do you have any suggestions as to which man should be nominated as chairman for the group this coming year?" Invariably I have said to them, "No, my nomination would be any one of the thirty-two [or thirty-six or forty, as the case might have been] men who are serving as deacons." I do not feel that any man should be allowed to serve as a deacon who is not also worthy of serving as chairman.

I am sure that I have special cause for thanksgiving when I remember the deacon chairmen that God has given to my ministry. Their faithful support of my pastoral leadership, their unfailing concern for the welfare of the pastor and his family, their willingness to share in the burdens of the difficult days, have been almost beyond belief and can be explained only by the grace of God.

Being asked to serve as vice-chairman of the group is also an expression of confidence. Holding this position should serve as a preparation period. As the name indicates, the vice-chairman should undergird the leadership of the chairman and be ready to step into the breach if the need arises, presiding in the enforced absence of the chairman. This officer should also carry that part of the detailed responsibility of the chairman which may be assigned to him.

The responsibility of the secretary of the deacons is not only to check the attendance of the men upon the meetings but to write the minutes of the deacons' meetings. I have seen some fearful things in the name of minutes. Not every deacons' meeting, of course, is as peaceful as another. There are differences of opinion, and there are expressions of such difference that ought to be forgotten before too long. To incorporate personal remarks into the record would simply be inexcusable. Many times I have had occasion to say to the secretary of the deacons sitting by me with his fountain pen poised, "This is off the record, you know." Minutes ought to reveal actions taken. They ought also to indicate the initiating of programs; evidences of progress should be found in the records. Personal remarks should not be included.

There are many occasions in the deacon activities when special committees are needed. Every deacon should feel the responsibility to serve when he is asked. I have often been amused in our deacons' meeting when some brother would bring up a matter that he considered of very vital import. Others would jump into the discussion, and soon someone would make a motion that a committee be appointed to look into this matter. Such a motion was almost a sure invitation for the individual making it to be chairman of the committee. Most of the time, the chairman looks around, and the brethren who have spoken most forcibly in favor of an idea are asked to do something about it. After all that is proper, is it not?

Fellowship.—One of the richest fellowships in a Baptist church is in the group of deacons actively serving the church. The church has made them a group. They are bound together by an unusual tie of service and responsibility. Men that were only casual acquaintances when they were made deacons have become fast friends. Men whose business interests vary widely find a common meeting ground in serving their church as deacons. A properly functioning deacon organization sees to it that opportunities for the development of this fellowship are many. Social periods for deacons and their families are very desirable. Some pastors think it worth while to have the deacons and their wives in their homes where this is possible. Fellowship is a thing to be highly valued and carefully cultivated.

The Scriptures say, "Bear ye one another's burdens, and so fulfill the law of Christ" (Gal. 6:2). This certainly applies to the close relationship that exists in the deacon group. In time of sorrow, deacons are quick to help each other and to offer a word of sympathy and of comfort. In time of sickness, they rally around and offer every aid possible. When a fellow deacon has slipped a bit in his way of life, it ought to be a deacon friend who comes to him first, sits down with him in a spirit of love, and tries to help. Occasionally, business reverses will come in the life of the deacon. His fellow deacons, with their own business contacts, will be among the first to know about it. They will also be among the first to offer a word of encouragement and such aid as is within their reach.

What does a deacon do? He does a lot in this new world of deaconship. There are these many things that he will be doing within the deacon group, a responsibility to the segment of the membership which is primary in his service.

THE HOUSEHOLD OF FAITH

A Baptist church is not first of all a program but a people. The church in the beginning was not an activity so much as it was a fellowship of the saved. The original seven deacons were called into service in relation to the membership of the Jerusalem congregation. They were to do something for the people and through the people. In extending and making more effective the ministry of the pastor, the deacons must of necessity deal with the church members. One of the most useful areas of service for the deacon is to carry some of the load of caring for the church family.

The group plan.—One of the most effective plans of organization for meeting this responsibility to the members is known as the group plan. This is the definite assignment of a certain number of the church families to each deacon's care for a year. To institute the system, make a careful survey of the church roll. All the people that live at one address are to be considered as one family. It may be that there are two or three groups at one address, or on the other hand, perhaps there is only one little child out of a family in which nobody else belongs to the church. Each address is to be considered a family unit. The number of families to be assigned each deacon is determined by dividing the number of deacons into the number of family units that there are in the church. It will be better to group the families for which a particular deacon is responsible in a given area. This makes for easier and quicker visitation.

The assignment necessitates a two-way relationship. That is, the deacon is given a list of the names and addresses for which he is to be responsible that year. He is to feel a special concern for them. In all questions that relate to this group, he will be the first man consulted. On the other side of it, the people in that group will be notified in a letter from the church who their deacon for the year is. They are given his address and telephone number and are urged to call him in case of any emergency where church aid is needed or church information desired. Thus the relationship which is to pre-

vail all year is established through the written assignment to
the deacon and the letters to his group before personal visitation begins.

Once the plan is established and the groups are assigned,
what is the deacon to do with this group of people during
the year? First, it will be a responsibility of visitation. Whatever the size of the church, it can do a tremendous amount
of good for every member to have a visit by a deacon during
the year. Some diligent deacons will visit their groups at
once after the assignment is made; others will be slower
about it. Visitation should be begun soon after the assignment of the list. It would be well if the deacon and his wife
could go together in the visitation of the home. Where as
many as fifty families are assigned to a man, it is not too
much to expect that these homes could all be visited in a
period of ten weeks.

This initial visit will be a "get acquainted" visit. Let the
deacon sit down with the family given to his care and talk
with them—talk about the church and the affairs of the
Lord. He should come to know the family and make its
members feel that somebody in the official life of the church
has a particular concern about them, their family, their
home, and their problems. Many a church member feels that
nobody cares about him or knows him. A prime purpose of
the visit is to make people know that the deacon is available
for service in the name of the church.

Let me insert a word of caution at this point, whether it is
needed or not. It sometimes happens that a church program
begins to revolve about the personality of the preacher. In
fairness, it must be said that this occurs many times when
the preacher desires it otherwise. The growth of the church
simply reflects the personal popularity of the pastor. Then
when the pastor is called away to another responsibility, as
often happens, what follows in the church is like pricking a

balloon. The program falters, and it becomes evident that the strength of the program was merely that of a personal relationship. It is entirely possible for this to happen in the dealings of a deacon with his group. The personality of the deacon and the warmth of his friendship make it possible for people to become more attached to the man than they do to the church. This is the thing, of course, which a deacon would not want and against which he can guard. Remember that the church program and responsibility is larger than any individual, either preacher or deacon.

In dealing with families in sorrow and in joy, a man will find that the tie becomes a very close one. People's hearts are opened in a peculiar fashion in such hours. God makes it a great opportunity for spiritual growth and kingdom advance. In those moments when the barriers are down and confidence is established, the deacon will have his greatest opportunity to tie a life and a home onto the church and into the progress of the kingdom of God. If the church provides a visitation card, the deacon should leave one upon this first visit with his phone number and address. People should be encouraged to call if they desire help from the church.

The church family census can be one of the finest projects under this group plan. One of the most profitable things ever done in my own church was to take a census of the church family through the visitation of the deacons. The deacons were asked, in going into the homes that had been assigned to them, to fill out a census card for every person found in the home. It was amazing to discover that in more than half of the homes, there was an evangelistic possibility. Perhaps it was a father or a mother or a child, perhaps a relative whose name was not even known. There are soul-winning opportunities for the church in many of its homes. Actually, it is almost the exception to find a whole family that belongs to the same church.

It is often discovered in this census that there are other families living at the same address who are evangelistic prospects or Baptists with church letters elsewhere. These can be added to the prospect roll of the church. This church family census should also provide the information that relates to the organizations of the church. How many members are enrolled in Sunday school, how many in Training Union, how many in Brotherhood, how many in the Woman's Missionary Union? In spite of the great growth of Sunday schools, it is still a fact that forty per cent of Southern Baptist church members are not enrolled. I have had a Sunday school enlargement campaign in my church based on this church census.

Still another discovery made possible by the church family census is that of the neglected and undiscovered talents that are in the lives of people. Here are members for the choir, teachers for Sunday school classes, leaders for the Training Union, and other workers. The other day I visited a fine Christian man who is soon to go home and be with the Lord. He told me that he had once been the director of the music as a paid worker in a Baptist church. Then he added, "Pastor, there is one thing that I have discovered for certain. If you have a talent and do not use it for the Lord it will soon be taken away from you." It is the church's responsibility and opportunity to discover these talents and see that they are dedicated to the life of the church. Church members will grow in grace in that dedication.

Visitation of the sick will be another project of the deacon in dealing with his group for the year. I believe that every pastor has a special heartache about this matter of the sick of the church family. To hear some people talk, one would think that the pastor was deliberately avoiding the sick or that he does not want to visit them. The condition of the church member simply has not been called to the pastor's attention in most cases. Once in a while, someone says, "Pastor, you didn't come to see me when I was sick."

My stock answer usually is, "Well now, that is strange. I must have mislaid that phone call from you, for the girls in the office didn't know anything about it. You did call me, didn't you?"

"Well, no, I didn't call."

"You called the doctor, didn't you?"

"Yes."

That line of conversation needs to go no farther.

The deacon can be a real help at this point. Dealing with a smaller group, acquainted with the pastor's viewpoint, and conscious of the fact that a good relationship between the pastor and the members is desirable for the sake of the church, he can make a real contribution by his own visitation. In the first place, he can be a source of information for the pastor about the sick. He also can screen the visits and indicate to the pastor which are more vitally necessary. Some people are really sick and others are simply enjoying poor health. There is a difference.

Now there are good and bad ways for a deacon to make a sick visit. Here is a good way to do it. Go out to make the call on a Sunday afternoon after having a little rest. After sitting down in the home of the church member, ask about his health and the welfare of the rest of the family. Then talk about the church, the services of the morning, and the blessings of God. These can always be discussed with profit. If the name of the pastor comes up in the conversation (it usually does), there is nothing to be gained by saying, "You mean the pastor hasn't been to see you!" When the pastor already has been there, such an expression of surprise is more appropriate, as, "Do you mean that the pastor was here! It is strange to me how he can get to so many places, as busy and responsible as he is, and yet that is just what he would like to do about every sick person." An effective service to the church certainly can be rendered at this point.

The door of the church.—In some areas of our country, the churches use the deacons to screen those desiring entrance into church membership. People who present themselves for membership in these churches are asked to meet with the deacons. In that meeting, they are asked to state their experience of grace, indicating that they have been converted and giving a history of their church experience, if any.

One summer, I visited a great Baptist church in New England. I noticed on the order of service that there was a "prudential committee." I learned upon inquiry that this committee met with all who desired membership in the church. It usually met just after the morning service. Having asked permission when the service was done, I went back to the room where the committee was meeting. The members waited for a little while and finally someone suggested that there was no one to interview that day and they might as well adjourn. I spoke to the person sitting beside me about the work of the committee and asked what would have been done had someone presented himself. She replied that those who came were asked to indicate that they had been saved. The inquiry would be directed towards the new birth. I heartily agreed with that and asked her if there would be any attempt to find out whether these people were really Baptists. In some confusion, she answered that of course there would.

There are many things to be commended in the plan. The point here is that the deacons are used for this purpose. The nature of their relationship to the church, their fellowship in service, and the spiritual qualifications which were present in them when they were selected by the church, all qualify them to be just that sort of inquiry group.

Church discipline.—It may be a little old-fashioned to introduce the idea of church discipline into this discussion, but after all, discipline is entirely scriptural. The Book says, "Withdraw yourselves from every brother that walketh disorderly" (2 Thess. 3:6). Traditionally in Baptist churches, the deacons have been the group charged with the responsibility of church discipline. Like many others, I grew up in the day when discipline was actually exercised, and it was not unusual at all for people to be called before the church to make explanations concerning their fashion of life.

A few years ago, I was conducting a meeting in a southern city. A woman came forward at the close of the service and said, as people will say to a preacher, "You don't remember me, do you?"

Well, after all these years I have learned the answer to that question. I said, "No, I don't remember you." She said that she had lived in a particular town in Oklahoma (where my father had been pastor while I was growing up) and then told me what her name had been before she had married. By mentioning her name, she wiped out about thirty years of my life, and I remembered a Wednesday night in the little church where my father was pastor. There was a church trial: a young woman was on trial, charged with playing the piano at a dance. I remembered her, and here she was after the years. We did not discuss that this time, but whenever I think of church discipline I remember many such church trials in which people were called to account.

A conscience on this matter of the kind of living by Christians that brings reproach to the name of the church is still needed. No group is better qualified to work in this area than the deacons. Paul's admonition is a good one to remember: "Brethren, if a man be overtaken in a fault, ye which are spiritual, restore such an one in the spirit of meekness; considering thyself, lest thou also be tempted" (Gal. 6:1). Discipline certainly is to be done in a spirit of love and understanding.

New members.—A fine deacon service in our church is that rendered to new members. Within two or three days after being received, every new member receives a letter from the pastor. This expresses a welcome and suggests that all who are officially connected with the church desire to be of service. It also says that in a few days, a deacon will call. The assignment of the names of the new members is made in rotation so that no deacon will be burdened more than another. The deacon visits in the home, talks about the program of the church, explains the services that are available to the member, and in every way seeks to make him feel at home. After he leaves the home, he makes a written report on the things that he has discovered about the family, its previous church background, the places of service which its members have occupied, and the things that they would desire to do in the life of our church. These visits have profited the church greatly.

Some deacon will say, "Well, that certainly is a fine program for deacons in a great city church, but there is little to do in our church with its membership of a hundred members, more or less." As long as these activities are considered in principle, they are applicable to churches of all sizes. The basic necessity for deacons in a small church is the same as it is in a large church. A revival would be introduced in many village and country churches if the deacons actually considered and accepted their responsibilities.

There is one problem in the smaller church that does not exist in the larger one. The deacons in a small church will represent a majority of the leadership in the congregation. If the church of a hundred members has four or five deacons, finding enough men who are qualified will gather the strongest leadership into one group. The strength of leadership and ability in such a group brings a temptation to rule rather than to serve. Remember that it is vitally important to approach being a deacon with a sense of service. The whole responsibility for the church life must be diligently shared with the people who have less ability, leadership, and opportunity. This problem is not so natural in the larger church, where there probably are just as many strong, capable men outside the deacon group as there are in it.

The nature of a man's service in a church as a deacon is the same. The nature of his selection is the same. His committal must have the identical quality of dedication. Regardless of the size of the church, it is the privilege of the deacon to preserve the identity of the individual in the life of his church. Being a deacon can be a full-time job; there is much to be done. There is an opportunity for a vast investment of life, but there are also promises of great rewards. The things that a deacon does can make his period of service the most wonderful experience of his life.

VI

THE DEACON AND THE
WORSHIP SERVICES

W ho has not played the "who's who game" when visiting
the services of another church? Games are not supposed
to be played in church, but there is something in the visitor
that makes him wonder who the people in the service are.
I went to church in New York City on one occasion, and a
man came out and began moving the pulpit and adjusting
the furniture. It was then time for the service to start. I
decided that he was the building superintendent but discovered in a few minutes that he was the pastor of this great
church. Is it possible to pick out the deacons in the service?
Are they easy to identify? If they are, what is it that sets
them apart?

There have been times in my ministry when I felt that we
had mistreated the deacons in the church and more particularly had done an injustice to the office of deacon. We had
not given to the office the proper recognition in our place of
worship. We had not made the men to know how responsible
they were and how important they were in the life of the
church.

I made a resolution on one occasion that when God should
call me to another church I would begin a new page in deacon relationships. The time soon came, and at our first meeting, I indicated to these friends that I would expect them
each Sunday morning and each Sunday night to meet me
just prior to the service for a period of prayer. Following

this, we would go out into the service together, and they could be seated on the front seats. They were too kind and courteous to "talk back," but I recognized that their reception of the idea was not totally happy. Some were wondering, no doubt, what their wives would say about sitting by themselves in the service. On the next Sunday morning, however, we began the practice with no spoken objections. This became one of the most productive elements in our whole program of worship before many months had passed.

As long as I served that church, I was made to know the importance of one step in the recognition of the deacon office. Soon the families of the men began to accept it and take proper pride in the fact that the husband or father had been set apart by the church to serve as deacon. The congregation was delighted to have an opportunity to determine that these were the men that had been selected and to become acquainted with them in their service. The deacons, like the preacher, became conscious of the fact that they must serve in the presence of the people; and that meant that they were responsible both to God and to the congregation.

Among other advantages, this practice makes it possible for the attendance of the deacons to be quickly improved. An absence from the front seat can be a very conspicuous thing. As I have said to my deacon friends in good humor, "Sitting there makes it mighty easy for the pastor to count you." More important, there is a wonderful feeling of strength that comes to the heart of the pastor when he looks down into the faces of these trusted men who are so vitally concerned about this service, the church, and the progress of the kingdom of God. However faltering the pastor's pulpit effort may have seemed, he can be quite sure that there is an undergirding foundation of prayer in the hearts of these men that will make his ministry more effective. I should like to offer a personal testimony that I cannot measure what the presence of the deacons at the time of the sermon has meant to my own ministry.

Later, in other pastorates, I have found it worth while to follow this same practice with different kinds of congregations. It has worked just as well with one as with another. It has lent a new dignity to the office of deacon and a new sense of responsibility to the man who fills it. It has taught church members about the sacred significance of the office that was first established by the wisdom of God and under the direction of the Holy Spirit. Thus, the first recommendation for what the deacon may do in worship is to occupy a position of public responsibility for the service.

The ordinances.—The deacon has a real part to play in other areas of the worship life of the church; his is not just a ministry behind the scenes or in the conference room. There is also a major opportunity in public, in the gatherings of the congregation. Remember that there are no specific tasks assigned to deacons in the Scriptures. They began with the serving of tables in a situation that was peculiar to the church at Jerusalem. These were the tables of benevolence and charity.

Custom, however, has assigned certain tasks to the deacons in Baptist churches, particularly with reference to the ordinances. The service of the Lord's Supper is commonly assigned to the deacons. I think that that is good. Each church will have its own plan as to time and method for the serving of the Supper. All would agree that the service ought to be conducted with dignity, that it ought to be done as an act of worship, that it is meant to be a memorial unto the Lord, and that the way it is done ought to constitute an honor and glory to his name.

The deacons will serve with dignity, but they are also responsible for preparation and planning. Many a pastor wants the chairman of the deacons to assist him in the serving. Where the congregation is large, there are many things to be done in the actual observance and where each deacon is to serve must be planned. It is not good to come to the service in which the Lord's Supper is to be observed and find that the men do not know the places of their assignment. The better the planning, the more meaningful the service.

The deacons may or may not be used in preparation and in assisting the candidates and pastor in the ordinance of baptism. In many churches, this practice is carefully followed. There are occasions when the pastor will need help in the administration of the ordinance. Occasionally, there will be a person who is an invalid that will require careful handling and extra strength. When someone is needed in the baptismal waters with the pastor, it is a good custom that one of the deacons be chosen for the task. Both of the ordinances, it should be emphasized, are under the authority of a New Testament church. Making a response to the will of the church in the administration of these two ordinances is the performance of a basic function.

Receiving the offering.—There are many things to commend the practice that is followed in so many churches of having the deacons receive the tithes and offerings at the worship service. It is a thing that needs to be done well and can be best done by an organized group. It also offers a fine opportunity to present the deacons at work in a public function. When the deacons are sitting as a group on the front seats immediately before the pastor, the receiving of tithes and offerings can be a beautiful and effective service. It will do away with the necessity of the long march down the aisle at the beginning of that part of the service.

The number of Baptist churches that have a tellers' committee is increasing. The responsibility of such a group is to count the money that is received by the church. This is not the place to discuss the committee as such but simply the deacon's relationship to it. If the deacons are to serve on it, the counting ought not to be done during the hour of worship.

A few years ago, I went to a church in a great city in the South to preach. As is my practice when I am at home, I arrived in time for the Sunday school service and spent a portion of the hour observing the school at work. There were many men whom I met that were serving as department secretaries and department officers that were presented to me as deacons. They were capable, aggressive, intelligent men of great leadership capacity. When I arose to preach in a little while, I missed many of these men that I remembered meeting. I inquired about their absence when the service was done, and it was explained to me that they were counting the money during the worship service. My reaction to that has never changed at all. A deacon may render a service by acting as a teller for the day, but the worship hour is to have a primary demand upon his presence.

Attendance.—There is nothing that the deacon can do concerning the worship service which will make the contribution that faithful attendance makes. It is tremendously important that the deacons be present. There simply is no substitute for faithful attendance. Remember that the preacher and the deacon are the only church officers mentioned in the New Testament. They have an equal responsibility in this matter of promoting the service of worship. The deacon has a special interest in the church program. He has been accorded a place of honor by the church and has a spiritual dedication to an office of great meaning to the church. He has something special to bring into the service of worship so his absence will be more than the absence of another member. Worship is a deeply spiritual exercise, and the deacon's

attitude makes a positive contribution towards the accomplishment of a worship experience.

I have a friend who is the pastor of a very large church.
A few years ago, he came to the prayer meeting service one
stormy Wednesday night to find that the weather had kept
all the people away—only he and the janitor were present.
The pastor was quite exercised about it and so expressed
himself to the janitor, the only one to whom he could express
himself. The janitor replied in inimitable fashion, "Yassuh,
yassuh, but I reckon we wouldn't be here if we wuzn't paid."
Attendance should not be professional, but there are rewards for being faithful to the responsibility that comes to
preachers and deacons alike of being present in the worship
services.

Greet the visitors.—In taking inventory of my own attitude, I believe that most people who visit a church tend to
sit in judgment on the hospitality of those with whom they
worship. I go away conscious of whether few or many people spoke to me. My people come back from their vacations
and talk about being present in services where nobody
greeted them. (Perhaps as visitors, we are partially to blame
ourselves.) Greeting visitors is a fine thing which the deacon
can do effectively. Just as soon as the service is dismissed,
he can move quietly through the congregation and be quick
to recognize the people who stand out as strangers. It will
mean much to a person to find that a deacon has sought him
out and is interested in the fact that he has been present in
the service.

When I try to insist upon my people doing this thing they
say, "But, Pastor, I don't even know the members. If I walk
up to a total stranger and tell him how glad we are to have
him, he is apt to reply 'Well, I've been a member here for
twenty-five years.'" It would need some discussion to know
whether the deacon or the person that is being greeted was

at fault in not knowing the other one. It certainly is true that if both have been members of the same church for twenty-five years and have not become acquainted, the hour is late and the time to begin is this particular service. Why not accept, as a responsibility of the deacons, the privilege of extending hospitable greetings to all who come into the worship service? It will mean much to the people that are greeted.

Ushering.—Ushering is a skill and an art. There are techniques which must be mastered if a man is to do an adequate job in this capacity. If the deacons are seated at the front as I have suggested, it would be impossible for them to serve as ushers and this particular discussion might be out of place. For the sake of those churches, however, that do not use this plan concerning the deacons in the services, it is readily apparent that no one could serve more efficiently as an usher than a deacon. No deacon should be satisfied, however, to be only an average usher. A careful study should be made of all the materials that are available to assist men in learning the art of ushering. A careful survey of one's own church situation as to the number of ushers needed and the most effective places for them to serve is also necessary. A few suggestions here will suffice.

First, do not allow the same person to be chairman of this group always. For the sake of developing other men, rotate the chairmanship. Likewise, do not leave men at the same position in the auditorium for every service. After they have served awhile at one point, move them to another. They will become acquainted with a new group of people and these people with them. Hold regular meetings of the ushers to discuss very frankly the good and the bad in what they have been doing. Ushering makes a real contribution to worship. It produces a frame of mind in the individual who comes to worship that either helps or hurts. It can mean much in the reverence which accompanies the service and is a part of the worship experience. If the deacons are to serve as ushers (which they can do most effectively), they are to accept this as a chief opportunity and responsibility in the worship life of the church.

The building.—The building committee of the church will be responsible for the building as to its cleanliness, temperature, and comfort. Deacons, however, as officials of the church are to have an interest in the building and take pride therein. If the building is not warm enough and no one is doing anything about it, the deacon should be the first one to arise quietly and see that something is done. All of the deacons should be alert to the details of the building appointments when they arrive on Sunday morning.

To wait until the service is under way to make criticisms or adjustments is to wait too long. It could be that it is the particular responsibility of some of the deacons to serve on the building committee and to tend to these matters that are suggested. Did the person responsible make proper distribution of songbooks in the auditorium, or are the lights that are on sufficient for the people to read and sing and enter into the service? It would not be practical to list all the details, but the point here is to call attention to the fact that the deacons should feel more than the average member's sense of responsibility regarding the worship service.

Responsibility for the pulpit.—The deacons have a special responsibility for the pulpit in the absence of the pastor. This does not mean that the deacons constitute the pulpit committee of the church by virtue of their office. Quite often the church has found it more practical to use a separate pulpit committee. In many cases the pastor himself is responsible for the supply of the pulpit in his absence, and this is quite good. There is another meaning entirely in speaking of the responsibility of the deacon for the pulpit.

It has been suggested that the deacon is responsible for the pulpit when the pastor is present. No preacher could say enough about how dependent he is upon those men closest to him, serving in this official, God-approved capacity. They pray so faithfully for the service and the work, for the will of God to be done in them. I like to believe that my deacons feel that my ministry in the pulpit at the hour of worship is a thing in which they are so vitally interested that they are also responsible. How much more then should the deacons feel that it is their special responsibility to pray for a visiting preacher when the pastor is away. How they should pray that God will overcome any difficulties created by a new voice at the hour of worship! If there can be such a thing as feeling an extra responsibility for attendance, I would certainly want it to be on the morning that the visitor is preaching.

Wednesday night deserves a special place in this discussion. Wednesday nights are not alike in all Southern Baptist churches. In some churches, there is a major service, and in others, one in a little room in a separate building. Traditionally, however, the Wednesday night service is a worship service in the life of the church. This time has been accepted as the midweek night for the church to worship for many years. The deacons in so many churches could lead the way in a rediscovery of the values of a midweek worship experience. I would not want to place an unfair burden on them about it, but the attendance of all the deacons would create a stir in an average Baptist church. The things that have been said about responsibility for the spirit and the results of worship apply equally to this Wednesday night service.

In describing Pentecost, the Holy Spirit said that Peter stood up with the eleven (see Acts 2:14). The word "with" here carries more meaning than the mere suggestion of geographical nearness. It is the translation of a New Testament Greek word which describes a fellowship that involves an identity of conviction, belief, action, concern, and faith. It means that all of the apostles were about to do the thing that Peter was about to do. It is one of the warmest and most intimate declarations of an identity of service in an hour of worship that can be found in all Scripture. This is also the relationship that exists between the pastor and his deacons. When the pastor stands up to preach or to lead the people in worship, the thirty-two (or whatever the number may be) also stand with the preacher. Though they may not arise from their seats, their hearts are warm with the same concern that is his. They desire to project the message effectively to the last person in the congregation just as the pastor is seeking to do.

The deacon's office is a public office as well as a private one. It is a service as well as a dedication of life. It is physical in its activity, and it is spiritual in its effectiveness. On Sunday morning or Sunday night or Wednesday night or in revival services, the worship opportunities of the church are the deacons' responsibility and challenge. When thinking of that which the deacons are to do, do not forget that there are things to be done in the presence of the people.

VII

THE DEACON AND CHURCH ADMINISTRATION

The atmosphere in the deacons' meeting had grown quite tense. It had all begun quietly enough with a discussion of the organization of the church, and in particular, who should serve on the finance committee. It had soon become evident however, that there was a wide difference of opinion about this particular committee.

Said one deacon, "We have the custom here in our church of a finance committee that is selected entirely from the deacons. This means that the organizations which spend the greater part of our local budget money, such as the Sunday school and the Training Union, often do not have direct representation on the finance committee. This is also true of the Woman's Missionary Union, which is a part of the total program of our church. It seems to me that it would be wise for us to have representatives of our various organizations on this committee, men from our deacons and altogether a group familiar with the purposes for which the church has said the money would be spent."

Replied a second deacon, "Well, I think we are getting along all right just as we are. After all, this is the thing that we are supposed to do as deacons. If we don't have sense enough to spend the church's money wisely then we ought not to be deacons."

A third deacon had this to offer, "We would do well to remember that the first deacons were called into being to transact the business of the church. Doesn't the Scripture say 'appointed over this business'? What are we supposed to do as deacons anyway?" The final question was really a good one, but it might have been asked in sincerity by half the membership of the church.

CHURCH BUSINESS

What is the deacon supposed to do about the business life of the church? Is not the management of that one of his primary functions? Every pastor remembers having people say to him, "I wish you would get the deacons to buy this or that." The general attitude of most churches would be that the business affairs of the church are largely in the hands of the deacons.

It ought to be said at once that this area of service offers unusual opportunities to a deacon who loves his church. There are no services which are particularly assigned to the deacons in the Scripture. It is customarily agreed, however, that the business area of the church is one in which the deacons may function to great advantage. This is true principally because within the deacons, churches usually have their most able men in financial and business judgment. Here are many men who themselves are owners of property or are familiar with economic conditions. By the nature of their lives, they are peculiarly equipped to care for the church business.

Then there is the passage in Acts that speaks of the original seven as being "appointed over this business." The deacon referred to above could have learned by careful examination that the word "business" in Acts is not synonymous with the financial life of a modern church. The men in Acts were to serve tables of benevolence. Theirs was a physical work of distributing that which had been brought for the supply of needy widows. The word which has been trans-

lated "business" actually means "need." In order to understand this need in the New Testament churches, it is necessary to study certain Scriptures.

Acts 2:44–45 says that the early Christians had everything
in common and provided for needy persons from the common fund. Acts 4:34–37 tells of Barnabas and others who
sold their possessions and put the proceeds into the common
fund. Acts 6:1–2 records the complaint about the distribution of the funds. An offering that was taken in various
churches for the poor saints at Jerusalem is described in Acts
11:29–30. The well-known passage about giving in 1 Corin-
thians 16:1–3 is related to this offering, and provides a regular plan for meeting the needs of the people. Second Corin-
thians 8–9 is devoted to the same subject. Paul's instructions
to Timothy about the kind of widows who were to receive
aid may be found in 1 Timothy 5:3–16. The primary emphasis in all of these passages is upon meeting the needs of the
people rather than upon the fact that deacons were responsible for handling the funds. Here it can be seen again that
the deacon's role is one of service.

At the same time, a basic qualification for a deacon is
having leadership ability and administrative possibilities.
These qualities can be used advantageously by a church,
and deacons should be used in the church's business affairs.
They are not the only ones to be used here, and this certainly is not their responsibility by divine right. It is an area
in which they can render a wonderfully fruitful and faithful
service.

Deacons must know first of all, that spiritual qualifications
are necessary to handle church business, money, and property in the right way. No man, even the president or execu-
tive officer of a large institution, is qualified by virtue of his
position in the secular world to take care of church business;
no man is qualified by virtue of the possession of vast wealth.

This is not said in a hostile spirit, but it must be said. There is an added endowment that is needed for dealing with the tithes and offerings that people have brought to be distributed according to God's will and for the advancement of his kingdom. Although God can use the abilities that have been developed through administrative and financial responsibility, spiritual qualifications are also necessary. A consecration of a man's capacities as developed in the things of the world to the things of God is necessary for the proper handling of God's business.

The reason for this is readily apparent. Money is not only money, and property is not only property. That may sound strange, but it reflects the truth that things which have been dedicated to God's use participate in, and partake of, two worlds. As an example, take a beautiful church pew. I would not know what it costs or what its property value is. The people who made it talked about the materials that went into it and the processes followed in its manufacture. They talked about the kind of finish that was put on it and other related matters. The pew is made from the materials of this world, and its manufacture is according to economic principles followed in this world. Yet it is a dedicated piece of furniture. Made for the accommodation of the worshiper, it is dedicated to the glory of God and has kingdom significance.

The Bible tells about the woman who had only two mites (about a penny) which she brought and put into the treasury of the Lord. Jesus was present on the occasion of her coming. Two mites could not be very important to the nation's economy. It would not normally be regarded as overly significant that a poor widow brought two mites to the treasury. Jesus said, however, that she had brought all that she had. He said that these two mites had a value beyond the understanding of any man of the world. They had spiritual significance. It is good for a person who is to handle God's business to have a wisdom concerning the things of this world and at the same time a wisdom concerning the things of God. These two put together make an unbeatable combination in transacting the business of a church. These are the two things which can most often be found in the lives of the deacons in a Baptist church. Dedication is really the key to a proper performance of this function.

Trustees.—It sometimes is wise for a church to select its trustees from among the deacons. In fact, this is quite common in Baptist churches. Some churches recognize the whole body of active deacons as the trustees of the church, and the officers of the deacons, by vote of the church, sign the church's legal papers. Trustees are not directors but simply the legal channels through which the will of the church is expressed. The need for correct legal procedure can be seen, for example, in the transfer of church property, where lawyers are quite concerned that the wording of a resolution to be adopted at a regular church business meeting will meet all of the requirements for title. Care in such action is proper and right according to Baptist pattern and tradition.

Finance committee.—Go back now to the matter of the finance committee with which the chapter began. The church mentioned there is not the only one in which the finance committee is made up entirely of deacons. Such committees are usually elected by, and responsible to, the deacons themselves. The deacons then assume the whole responsibility of finances for the church.

Although it is a good and safe custom for the deacons to be well represented on the finance committee, it is not the best practice to exclude all others. There are men who could not qualify, at least at the time, for election as deacons who could serve effectively on this committee and receive valuable training in so doing. Another important reason for including people who are not deacons is the need for having someone present in the committee meeting who can discuss an item that comes up for explanation. When a question is raised about a particular disbursement, someone should be there who knows the reasons for it. Thus it is good for the Sunday school superintendent, the Training Union director, and the presidents of the Woman's Missionary Union and the Brotherhood—or some other representatives of these organizations—to be members of the finance committee.

Remember that the finance committee and the deacons are not policy making bodies. Certainly a recommendation from this important committee will be received by the church with as much seriousness as one from the deacons. Both the deacons and the committee, however, are meant to carry out the expressed policies of the church. The budget is the expressed will of the church concerning the distribution of funds.

Although distribution is the responsibility of the church, the practice of having a committee to plan a budget for expenditures has proved wise. In fact, the finance committee may do this. In churches where the committee is rightly constituted in personnel, this is the reasonable thing to expect. It will therefore make a survey of the history of church spending and the needs of the church program. The recommendations for enlargement will come from the pastor and from others. Putting all the information together, it will recommend a budget to the church which will serve as a covenant of distribution for the new year. The church will discuss this frankly, each member will have an opportunity to know about it, and finally the desire of the church will be expressed in a vote.

Church property.—The upkeep of the church property, though commonly assigned to a committee established for that purpose, is a matter in which the deacon should take an unusual interest. As with the finance committee, deacons will serve on this committee. Something is wrong with a deacon who does not take pride in the fact that the property of the church is rightly kept. A group of spiritual, church-selected men would not al' ɔw God's house to be less well kept than their own homes. Cleanliness and repair are both included in such an admonition.

By way of summary, the area of business and church property is one in which the deacon is peculiarly fitted to render an unusual service. Only the fact that he is a spiritual and a dedicated man would enable him to understand that he is to carry out the will of many people who in a business sense have neither the wisdom nor the experience that has been given to him. The need for this warning may be especially great in smaller churches.

In my first pastorate, there was a deacon who, almost alone in the church, was a man of substance and property. He was a wonderful Christian, honest, retiring, devoted to his church and to his pastor. At one point, however, he always met great difficulty. Many times he has said to me, "Pastor, it just doesn't seem right to me that we should carry our policy before the church concerning the distribution of the money and allow an eleven-year-old child to have the same vote as anybody else. What could those children know about the spending of money for the purchase of property or the repair of property or any one of many things which we do that require business experience?"

Each time I would explain to him that the money of the church had peculiar and special significance as the spiritual property of God. These children who voted upon church policies were children who had professed faith in Jesus and had, as far as we could know, an experience of grace. This meant that the Holy Spirit would lead them just as he would lead adults. The maturity and experience of the older Christians would be used of the Spirit in any decision reached. The end result would be the will of God, which is always primary.

THE CHURCH PROGRAM

"Program" has almost become a technical word with Baptists. It suggests the projection of new ideas with supporting propaganda. It is not in that sense, however, that I want to use it. Let the word stand for the organized activities in which the church engages. What is the program of a New Testament church? It is carrying out the Great Commission. Every organization and every activity should have scriptural justification in the Great Commission. Jesus said, "All power is given unto me in heaven and in earth. Go ye therefore, and teach all nations, baptizing them in the name of the Father, and of the Son, and of the Holy Ghost; teaching them to observe all things whatsoever I have commanded you: and, lo, I am with you alway, even unto the end of the world" (Matt. 28:18–20). No one would question the size or the eternal significance of this challenge which Jesus gave to his disciples. We Christians march as those commanded by a sovereign, and there is no escape from the fact that the world must be reached with our witness. The one inescapable responsibility and privilege of the deacon, therefore, is with reference to this program of the church embodied by the Great Commission.

Evangelism.—Each New Testament church ought to have a program of evangelism. Men and women are to be made disciples. This is the basic responsibility of all churches. The deacon is to feel a first responsibility then for this major task of his church. The deacon needs to be a personal soul-winner. If the deacons and the preachers are not soul-winners, the people cannot be expected to be.

Many say, "I just cannot do that." The Bible teaches that anybody can be a soul-winner who has been saved. It does not anywhere suggest that it is easy. From my experience as a preacher, I doubt that anyone finds soul-winning easy. It certainly has not been proved so in my own life. But every deacon, every preacher, every member of the church can and ought to be a personal soul-winner. We should care that people are lost. Compassion should be the keynote of a deacon fellowship. In remembering that the deacon was to extend the effectiveness of the ministry, I feel that there is nothing that more undergirds the work of the pastor than a group of men whose hearts are warmed and concerned for a lost world.

The deacons, with the pastor, ought to see to it that the church has a planned program of evangelism. God intends for Christians to be intelligent about their approach to a lost world. A great city church or a part-time rural church should have a definite, basic plan of evangelistic endeavor. The deacons, by reason of their dedication and interest, are fitted more than anyone else to provide this plan and to promote it vigorously in the church. Such a plan would include perennial evangelism, which means the winning of people to Christ from service to service and from Sunday to Sunday. Is it not a wonderful thing for a deacon in the church that has services only once a month to be able to say on the day for the services, "Pastor, these people have been won during the month since we saw you last and will be ready to come forward at the service and make personal confession of their faith."

Lost people are to be found in any community. It is a demonstrated fact that in every place in Southern Baptist territory there are some people without Jesus. Planned, perennial evangelism involves knowing who these people are and where they live. Some deacon groups have blessed a church greatly with a weekly plan of visiting the lost. A night in the week is selected when church members go out two by two to try definitely to win somebody to Jesus. Those who are won are encouraged to come to the house of the Lord on the very next Sunday and to profess their faith.

Besides the program of perennial evangelism, there is the program of mass evangelism which every church follows. This means at least one revival meeting a year, and in many churches, two or three. I still believe in mass evangelism. I believe the Bible teaches mass evangelism and that mass evangelism centers in the church. Even in his own day, Jesus' followers were prone to run off after strange leaders. There are some deacons and even some pastors in this day who, in the name of evangelism, give much loyalty and much effort to a man who is unattached and almost unidentified. Mass evangelism ought to center in the churches in order to produce fruit in the churches. It is this that makes it a deacon's responsibility.

The deacon can render fine service in this program of evangelism by the organization of prayer groups that fit in with the rest of the life of the church. Prayer, compassion, personal witnessing, and mass evangelism are all parts of the same program. Each deacon and each pastor would want to take a personal inventory from time to time, asking himself, "What part am I playing in winning people to Jesus through the witness of my church?"

The organizations.—The organizations of Baptist churches have been brought into being by the compulsion of their evangelistic commission. In Southern Baptist life, the organizations form the very heart blood of the church next to the worship service. The blessings that God has showered upon these organizations are amazing. They are not perfect, just as there is a lack of perfection in all things in this world. There is every evidence, however, that these organizations were brought into being through the leadership of the Holy Spirit.

They have enjoyed a phenomenal growth. Many of the achievements that have come as churches have sought to carry out the Great Commission and win the world to Jesus have been made possible through the channels of these organizations. There are four basic units: the Sunday school, the Training Union, the Woman's Missionary Union, and the Brotherhood. The church that does not have all of them should ask itself if it could. Are there enough people to lead them? Is there enough interest to support them? The deacons will be able to provide the best answers to these questions, and they should be the first to recognize the need.

The deacon has a responsibility to each one of these organizations. First, he has the personal responsibility which any church member has that is committed to the thing the church is set up to do. He also has a special responsibility as a man who is a dedicated leader, expected in the Scriptures to be an example in the life of the church.

A great deal of emphasis is needed at this point. Many deacons simply do not realize how important they are to the success of the organizations within the church. *The least that a deacon can do is to have membership in all of the organizations of the church which are designed for him.* It is indeed a tragedy to have a deacon in the church that does not go to Sunday school when he is physically able to attend. A man need not talk about supporting the organizations of his church if he does not show up when they meet. There is no real support without attendance; absence serves to give an organization a polite burial. There is one vote that can always be cast for Jesus and his church by the person who is able to, and that is the vote that is cast by attending the church's services. On the other hand, there is the negative vote as easily cast—the blackball of absence.

1 have a friend in the community in Arkansas where I used to be pastor. He would often say to me, "Preacher, I tell you, you are doing a marvelous work. I just want you to know that I appreciate it and that I am for you all down the line."

The trouble was that this was a sort of absentee vote of confidence. I would say to him, "You know, Nick, all of those nice things that you are saying sound so good to me that I could believe them if I could just look into your eyes about eleven o'clock on Sunday morning when I stand up to preach." He would take it in good humor and assure me that he meant to do better about it. In the years since I lived there, I have visited with him and have discovered to my joy that he is indeed doing something about it.

It is possible for a group of deacons in a church to remake and revitalize the Baptist Training Union program. A very efficient deacon chairman in a church where I was pastor undertook to keep up a census of the deacons' activities. Each month in making his report to the deacons of their work, he would report on their enrolment in Sunday school and Training Union, and their attendance of the worship services, thus challenging them to greater participation in the work of the church. There are some churches where consternation would reign supreme if every deacon would show up on a Sunday night to enrol in Training Union. If this were to happen, however, each deacon enrolling would find that he had influenced many other people to see their responsibility for training in church membership.

This discussion, of course, does not mean that the deacons who do not attend the Training Union, the Wednesday night service, or some other organized activity are actively opposed to it. As a matter of fact, if the question of continuing a particular activity were brought to a vote in the church, these men would be the first to vote in favor of continuing it. The problem lies in the fact that the activities need more than vocal support. Each organization and each service needs the kind of vital, demonstrated loyalty that manifests itself in attendance and positive interest. It is certainly God's plan that the preaching service is to be central in the life of the church, but the organizations and other services have a vital role in supporting, building, and contributing to this great, central experience of worship.

Not only can the deacons render a service by being a part of the organizations of the church, but most of them will carry some special responsibility in those organizations. This almost goes without saying, because deacons have leadership abilities. Once they give themselves to attending an organization, they are soon given responsibility for leadership in it. It does not seem wise for one man to hold a major place of leadership in more than one organization. If, for example, he is to be a superintendent in the Sunday school, it will not often be wise to have him as a director in the Training Union also. The man holding a major office in one organization, however, can hold one of smaller responsibility in another one. In view of their leadership capacities, the deacons' positive support in all of the organizations which contribute to basic objectives of the church will mean much toward the church's growth and the effectiveness of its ministry.

Serving on committees.—Another opportunity for the deacon to serve is found in the committee plan which most churches use today. While varying with the size of the church, there will be such committees as the Lord's Supper, baptism, property, grounds, benevolence, finance, nominations, pulpit supply, and many others. To these various groups are delegated the responsibilities of the church. Deacons should serve on all of these. The committees are not necessarily to be deacon committees, but the wisdom, experience, and dedication of the deacons ought to be a part of their operation. Every deacon will be willing to serve on these committees as his services are requested.

Here are some principles upon which we build the committee work in our church. The first one is that no man shall serve on more than one committee each year. The committees all meet on the same night each month in line with this principle. Committee-meeting night for us means that at 6:45 in the evening the chairmen of the committees meet with the pastor for thirty minutes. Then the committees themselves are in session for the next forty-five minutes. After that, the deacons meet in their monthly meeting. One night is made to serve the whole planning responsibility of the church.

The second principle is that no man shall serve as chairman of the same committee two years in succession. In addition to that, we do not have the person to serve more than two years on the committee whether chairman or not. This makes it possible to use many people in the program. It also encourages the use of a man in different places of responsibility. The more places he serves, the more acquainted he becomes with what actually goes on in the life and program of the church. There is enough work right here to keep every deacon busy and growing in his understanding of the many-sided features of our program.

Stewardship.—The distribution of tithes and offerings has been discussed in the section on the finance committee. The stewardship program of the church is actually something entirely different. It involves the responsibility of the individual to the Lord in the matter of the things committed to his care. Every Christian is a steward. No church is faithful to its task that does not teach this to the people and provide a challenge for the most effective stewardship. What is the source of the financial strength of a New Testament church?

The scriptural answer is tithes and offerings. The tithe is the minimum, the starting place and anything less than the tithe, the Bible says, is dishonest. Malachi said, "Will a man rob God? Yet ye have robbed me. But ye say, Wherein have we robbed thee? In tithes and offerings" (Mal. 3:8). Many people actually do not tithe and become dishonest stewards because a church has failed to teach biblical stewardship effectively. The pastor and the deacon will provide the first example of being faithful in the matter of the tithe. A covetous preacher or a covetous deacon can almost wreck a program of stewardship in the church.

Stewardship teachings also include emphasis upon the fact that the tithe is to be brought into the storehouse. The only storehouse mentioned in the New Testament is a New Testament church. The tithe is to be brought to the church undesignated, to be distributed by the will and vote of the church. This is tremendously important for many reasons. It enables a Christian to get himself out of his giving. It is awfully easy to say "my tithe." It is just as easy to insist on what should be done with the tithe. This only serves a selfish purpose. When the tithe is brought to the church in obedience to the command of Jesus and its distribution is left in church hands, it is the church's tithe, not "mine." The glory, therefore, is not to the individual but to the church, which is scriptural and right. Deacons and preachers will be the key men in this basic New Testament program.

Missions.—All spreading of the gospel at home or abroad is missions. Everything that is done at home or elsewhere to contribute to the Christian witness must be so considered. Paying the light bill of the church or the janitor or the pastor, keeping the church in repair, and sending missionaries to a foreign field are all part of the same enterprise. The word "missions" has become a geographical term, but it was never that with Jesus. The concept of the Scripture is the gospel for the whole world, and anything less than that is too little. No church has a right to exist that is not large enough to have the whole world in its heart. Deacons are the men who along with their pastor will lead in maintaining this world concept of Christian witnessing. It is so important to maintain a balanced perspective in considering all the needs of the kingdom.

The great channel of Southern Baptist missions outside the local church is the Cooperative Program. In spite of all of our designated gifts, it remains true that the Cooperative Program is the channel that keeps our mission enterprise alive. The deacons will see to it in their recommendations and in their planning with the church that the whole world is included in the church covenant of distribution.

Building programs.—Building a church building is not simply a local project, for it too has mission significance. No church's building is as large as its task. There are very few Southern Baptist churches whose auditoriums are large enough to seat half of their memberships. We Baptists confess by the size of our buildings that we do not expect our people to attend church with regularity. I have often wondered what it would be like to have all the members of my church to attend the service on the same Sunday morning. I expect one thing that would happen would be that the shock would nearly kill me. There might have to be a preacher funeral on Monday. The other thing would be that half of the people would have to stand in the street, for the church did not really expect them. Deacons are the men who will have the vision of God in this matter of church buildings. Buildings must not be built to the neglect of mission fields, but buildings are part of the mission program.

What does a deacon do in the life of a church? If he tried to do all the things which have been discussed in these past chapters, he would not only have to give up his vocational responsibilities, but he would need to become at least three men to project his life into all these areas. The deacon is to be a busy man. There are infinite opportunities of service in both small churches and large. His usefulness and leadership are really unlimited. In the fellowship of his own group, throughout the membership of the church in visitation, in the worship life of the church, in the work of all the organizations, in the program, the deacon can be busy all the while and can become that which God has purposed for his service.

VIII.

THE DEACON'S FAITH

Then there arose certain of the synagogue, which is called the synagogue of the Libertines, and Cyrenians, and Alexandrians, and of them of Cilicia and of Asia, disputing with Stephen. And they were not able to resist the wisdom and the spirit by which he spake" (Acts 6:9–10). Stephen, as a deacon, was a man of fixed convictions. He believed something and the thing that he believed actually determined the fashion in which he died. He is an excellent illustration of the fact that a deacon is to be a man of deep personal convictions in his faith.

One of the qualifications for a deacon found in the third chapter of 1 Timothy is that he holds "the mystery of the faith in a pure conscience" (1 Tim. 3:9). Mystery, in the New Testament, means "revealed secret." It is a reference to the full revelation of God which is in Christ Jesus. The Christian's creed is that which he believes about Christ. The deacon is to hold this in his heart unswervingly as the basic fact of his being. One commentator has put it, "It was not the function of a deacon to teach or preach; it was sufficient if he were a firm believer." First Timothy 3:13 speaks of the deacon as having "great boldness in the faith."

Nothing is more important in the deacon's life than what he believes. This alone can stabilize his deaconship and give depth to his service. There is a great difference between a man's opinions and his convictions. An opinion is an idea that he holds, while a conviction is an idea that holds him. It was that which those early Christians believed that en-

105

abled them to speak with great boldness when their very lives were at stake. What they believed enabled them to die as they did like heroes and heroines of the faith. Their faith was contagious. Nothing else could account for the spread of Christianity until it enveloped their world.

What a deacon believes is important because it will determine the kind of life he will present to the world. It will measure his loyalty to Christ, his church, his denomination, and his people. It will be the source of genuine compassion for a lost world. Because of the place that he occupies, it will be peculiarly significant in the lives of others. No deacon in a Baptist church can possibly be what he ought to be unless he is well grounded in the truth as Baptists believe it and is loyal to it.

A deacon in a Baptist church ought to be a true Baptist. That is no hardship for any Baptist church member. Baptists hold to the New Testament as their sole guide in faith and practice and believe that each one may read and interpret it for himself. They believe that putting a New Testament into the hands of a saved person and asking him to read with an eye single to the kind of a church that is described in its pages will lead him to become a Baptist. A lesser conviction than that can unfit a man to serve as deacon.

In many Baptist churches, the deacon is examined publicly before being ordained to his office, as is the custom in ordination to the ministry. As a matter of actual necessity, it has already been determined by the man's life in the church that he believes the things which he ought to believe as a deacon. The examination is not primarily to instruct him or to decide whether or not he will be able to pass the requirements. It does often serve as a helpful witness before the church to the things which Baptists "most surely believe." Some churches have abandoned this practice of public examination. In either case, it is important that the church understand that the man's beliefs play a vital part in his fitness for the office of deacon.

Many books are available about Baptist doctrines, and this discussion cannot review all of them. There are some basic doctrines which every deacon must believe. Surely a deacon is well grounded in his belief about God the Father; about the Son, his virgin birth, his sinlessness, his atoning death, his resurrection, and his promised return. He will recognize the Holy Spirit as the third and equal member of the Godhead who comes to bring all things to the Christian's remembrance concerning Christ. The Bible to him is God's inspired Book. It is altogether true, the rule of faith and practice.

There are, however, certain doctrines in some degree distinctive with Baptists that will, in the measure they are heeded, determine what kind of deacon a man becomes.

Salvation.—It is essential that a deacon be well grounded in the doctrine of salvation both by experience and precept. Salvation is by grace, not by works. "For by grace are ye saved through faith; and that not of yourselves: it is the gift of God" (Eph. 2:8). Salvation in Christ Jesus is the gift of God to every repentant, believing sinner. Then, salvation is not by church membership. There is no saving efficacy in the ordinances. They are not sacraments, and they are not channels of saving grace. It likewise follows that infant baptism is not scriptural and has no saving power. The Holy Spirit works a new birth in the heart when one is saved, and one becomes thereby a child of God. Because God does the saving, not man, salvation is eternal, for God could not do a thing imperfectly. As Christians, we are in fact become new creations in Christ Jesus when we believed in him.

Few indeed are the deacons that would be otherwise minded about this doctrine. For an effective service in the churches of our Lord, a man must be able to say for himself "one thing I know." Baptists preach an experiential gospel. This thing has happened to us and therefore we can speak of it with authority. Possessed by this conviction and proved by this experience, the deacon is able to be a good witness and a personal soul-winner.

The New Testament church.—More emphasis is needed on that which the Scriptures teach concerning a New Testament church. This church was founded by Jesus himself while he was here. As he said, "Upon this rock I will build my church; and the gates of hell shall not prevail against it" (Matt. 16:18). It did not begin at Pentecost; it was not an aftermath of his ministry. In the wisdom of our Lord and in the purpose of God, it came into being while Jesus was here. The New Testament church is a local visible body of baptized believers banded together for the proclamation of the gospel.

All authority in a New Testament church resides in the congregation under the headship of Christ. This means that there is no episcopacy by which the preacher is to have the authority in the church, nor is there any system of orders by which the authority becomes a part of the deacon office. People received into the membership of the church must be voted upon by the church itself as the keepers of the membership. Likewise people commended to another church are recommended by the vote of the congregation. Programs and policies are, in the final sense, church programs and church policies. This conviction concerning authority makes a very basic difference between Baptist churches and most other denominations. As a part of such church convictions, the preachers and deacons become in truth servants of the church, absolutely dedicated to doing the will of the church.

A deacon not only ought to believe that this is true about the church but that it is also wise and right. Is it necessary so to speak? Far too many Baptists give lip service to this doctrine, recognizing that God really teaches it, but feel deep down that there ought to be a better way. It is necessary to believe that because God teaches it, his wisdom is to be found in giving to a congregation of baptized believers the authority of the group.

This is the reason that Baptists are essentially a "meeting" people. We need to get together in order that the congregation may reach a common conclusion as to the will of God. During the course of a twenty-five-year ministry, I have attended thousands of Baptist meetings. My preacher father told me when I first started preaching always to go to the meetings. He said that many of them would leave me feeling that they were fruitless but that in all of it, God was working wisely to accomplish his will and his purpose. The years have proved that that is exactly true. Blessings are to be found in the gathering of the people in order that as a congregation, they may exercise the authority God has granted to such a congregation.

In these meetings, I have heard many brethren express themselves, saying that the church ought to express itself. In the deacons' meeting, assent is given to the idea that church approval is necessary for any newly-conceived program or project. The fact remains that the idea could arise that this is just a formality through which Baptists go. Each member of the church has access to the leadership of the Holy Spirit and consequently has a right to speak. The pastor of the church surely has no more access to God's leadership than does any other converted sinner. Perhaps the basic reason that underlies all that I have said about authority is the fact that all of us need again and again to realize that the wise course for saved people is found in the will of God. This will is made known to his people, though often in unexplained ways, and is always proved to be the best.

It is well to have a conviction about the New Testament church that harmony in the church is not simply to be desired but is divinely commanded. In fact, anything short of that is heresy. The oft-repeated phrase that Baptists can be recognized because they are "fussy" is provocation for righteous indignation. The devil started that, and it is a bit of his ingenious propaganda. There is nothing religious or Christian about a fuss, nothing at all. Harmony is the New Testament pattern; it is the Spirit's desire. A departure from harmony is a departure from the will of God and is therefore sin.

This does not mean "peace at any price." It does not involve a compromise with wickedness and with the devil. It sets up a New Testament ideal for which the preacher and the deacon and each member of the church will actively and consistently strive. It warns of the pitfall that can rob a church of its power and rob duly chosen leaders in the church of their effectiveness and usefulness. Harmony is a scriptural must.

The Scriptures also teach that a New Testament church is a "blood-bought institution." It was so characterized by Paul as he spoke to the Ephesian elders (Acts 20:28). Thus the price that Jesus paid for our redemption is linked with the founding of New Testament churches and their basic purpose in the world. Such a blood-bought institution becomes deserving of the first loyalty of each member and is unlike any other institution in the world. Loyalty is to be sought without an apology. The right kind of deacons will expect the members of the church to be loyal. It is unthinkable that a man in this position would go out to invite people to his church with apology in his heart and on his lips. There is no need to make excuses for people even before they have opportunity to speak for themselves. I have learned that they are all well able to make their own.

One of the finest deacons that I have ever had the privilege of knowing had one little chink in his armor. If the lecturer at the Grand Lodge was to be in the city on a Wednesday night, I could resign myself to the fact that my deacon probably would not be at church. When it came to a choice between his lodge and his church on Wednesday night, he would make the wrong choice. There are far greater sins, to be sure; but it does indicate something short of the hundred per cent loyalty that a man owes to the only divine institution in the world.

This particular deacon reminds me of the old story about the two men (as some tell it, they were deacons) who were out possum hunting on a Wednesday night. After a few hours had gone by, they were sitting on a log, enjoying the fellowship of such an occasion. One of the men suddenly remembered that it was Wednesday night and said to his friend, "John, do you realize that this is prayer meeting night at the church?"

Answered his friend, after a moment's disconcerted silence, "It really is, isn't it?" Then his face brightened as he said, "But Jack, that's all right; I couldn't have gone to prayer meeting anyway. My wife's sick tonight."

A New Testament church, founded by Jesus and operating under his personal headship, deserves everyone's greatest loyalty. Disloyalty to the church is disloyalty to Jesus.

Money.—If it seems that too much has been said about the deacon and his money, take another look at the New Testament and find how much more the teachings of Jesus concern money. There are some things which a deacon should believe about money that can make all the difference in his service. First, it is important for everyone to understand that the money which each one has is not his own; it belongs to God. "Know ye not that . . . ye are not your own? For ye are bought with a price" (1 Cor. 6:19–20).

Starting at this point and recognizing God's ownership of all money makes it far easier to tithe and handle all money according to God's will.

This understanding will enable the deacon to spend the rest of the money after the tithe is brought to his church on the things that will please God. It will guard him against covetousness. The place of beginning, then, is in recognizing that all money belongs to God. The Scriptures tell us that the cattle on a thousand hills are his and the silver and gold are all his. They teach that it is God that gives the power to get wealth.

Two or three things will help in understanding this basic conviction. Remember how quickly money can be taken. If anyone, preacher, deacon, or member, has a covetous heart, he ought to take the warning of the Scriptures and of life that it is very easy for God to solve that matter and take all of one's possessions. Someone has said that God is a very good collector. The Bible clearly teaches that the wrong use of money leads to disaster in life.

Once I was called back to a town, where I had previously been pastor, to conduct the funeral of a prominent man in the little town. He had not been a member of my church or of any church in the city, but we had been business friends. I was a friend of the family. When I arrived the evening before the service, I went down to the house to see the members of the family and the friends that were dropping by during the evening. Since he had been a very prominent man in the community, many people were gathering and coming and going. Surely the gathering of a community in an hour of sorrow like that, to make expression of its sympathy, is one of the sweetest experiences, sweetest privileges of living in a small town. I walked up on a conversation between three men during the evening. Just as I joined them, one of the men said to another, "How much did he leave?"

One of the other two most effectively closed the conversation by replying, "All that he had."

It is well for the deacon to recognize that the church money does not belong to a church officer or to an official church group but is first the Lord's and then the congregation's to distribute under the leadership of the Holy Spirit. It is indeed easy for good men to get a sense of proprietorship about money which is not theirs, although it has been given into their care. Some will find a joy in writing a check for an organization that they might not be able to write on their own accounts. I once heard a church treasurer (not from my church, I am grateful) say, in disagreeing with a disbursement upon which the church had insisted, "Well, I can attend to that; I'll just not write the check." This man, of course, does not represent the average treasurer in a Baptist church. Treasurers are a group of fine, godly, dedicated people. The authority of the church must always extend into every realm of its operations. No one by reason of his office is to be a checkrein or to exercise a veto upon the will of the church as it sets forth its program and instructs its committees. The tithe brought to the church ceases to belong to the one who brings it.

The preacher.—What does a deacon believe about the preacher? More important, what does God say about the preacher? Since the relationship of the deacon is so intimately connected with that of the preacher, the deacon's conviction here will be important in the quality of his service. The Bible teaches that the preacher has a peculiar call from God that is directly to the ministry. There are many people in the world who believe that the calling of all men and women in their vocations is the same as God's call to religious vocations. This is debatable ground, but it seems obvious from the Scriptures that there is a definite call for the preacher. A deacon should be mindful of that.

The relationship between a pastor and a church should be a Holy Spirit–directed relationship. No preacher has a right, when a church has no comparable impression, to say, "The Holy Spirit tells me to work with you, and I am therefore to be your pastor." The Spirit's leadership works on both ends of the line when it concerns more than one individual. No preacher would want to be the pastor of any church without the thorough-going conviction that that was the will of God for him. Neither would he want to be pastor of a church in which this conviction had not been supported by a like impression upon the hearts and minds of the congregation. The happy pastorate is one in which God has spoken to a church and to a man, and man and church have been brought together in spiritual union.

When the deacon thinks of the preacher in the light of New Testament teachings, there ought to be a conviction that God has created the office of deacon in order that it might make the pastor's ministry more effective. I have already suggested that I am indebted to deacons more than any preacher I know. They have done more for me at this very point than I would have dreamed possible. They have been as patient with my impatience, they have been as kind in their teaching, and as constant in their helpfulness as any preacher on earth could have desired. This was the way God intended it. The deacon should uphold and extend the ministry of the man that God has called to serve as pastor.

We pastors certainly are not infallible. It is quite possible for us to be selfish. With all of that, it is one of the most dangerous things in the world to the spiritual usefulness and spiritual life of a deacon to be brought into a place where he feels that he must oppose the leadership of the man that God has called as his pastor, even when such opposition is justified by the circumstances. God himself will deal with the situation if he is given the opportunity.

I have often read that passage in the Old Testament about when David went down to the camp of King Saul and his chief man went with him. God caused a deep sleep to fall upon the camp of Saul. Saul, who had been following David so mercilessly, was sleeping in a trench in the middle of his men, when David and his chief lieutenant came upon him. The lieutenant said, "Let me smite him."

David answered, "No, we cannot do that."

"If you will just let me smite him once, there will not be a second time."

But David was firm. "God will not hold him guiltless that lifts up his hand against the Lord's anointed." There certainly was no time for a long theological discussion that night between David and his lieutenant, but I think David might have said to him, "I am aware of his wickedness. He is the Lord's anointed, but he is a braggart and a boaster. He has defied God and sinned against him. He has refused to do what God commanded about the Amalekites. He has pursued us with hate in his heart. But even so, because he is God's selected man, I must leave him in the hands of God for judgment."

Some of the finest men that I have known in this world bore the scars of controversy in which their deacon responsibility had come into conflict with the pastor's office. In most cases they had been really justified, but it would have been better for their ministry had they left the judgment to God.

In a school on deacons one evening a slip of paper was passed forward with the question on it, "Does the Board of Deacons have the right to declare the office of pastor vacant?" The answer is a little elementary. It must be no, for the church alone has the authority to declare the pulpit vacant. Neither the deacon nor the pastor holds a position of authority. Both are elected servants of the church. The deacons can and certainly ought to offer constructive, loving

criticism and advice to the pastor. It is fine when the rela
tionship between the two is such that such things can be
discussed and a spiritual fellowship prevail.

I was succeeded in a pastorate by a personal friend who is
a very capable, dedicated, good man. Things did not go too
well for him in the first months of his pastorate. One day I
received a telephone call from a man in the town who told
me that he had learned that I was to speak in a neighboring
community twenty miles away on the next evening. He
asked me as a personal favor to stop to see him when I
passed through the town.

"You would like to talk to me about something personal?"
I asked.

"Yes," he replied, "it is something in which I need you
personally."

"Then I certainly will do it."

When I arrived the next afternoon at the man's office, he
had gathered a group of men from the church to be there.
To say that I was disappointed is putting it mildly, for I was
really a little bit hurt. I was grieved that they thought that
I would have any part in a conference in which they wished
to discuss their pastor. One man who set himself up as
spokesman told me the things that were problems with them
about the pastor. None of it was really important. He even
thought that the preacher preached too long, and I remembered that it was his custom to sleep half through the sermon
anyway.

Finally I said, "Jim, when did you last pray for your pastor?"

He grew a little pale, then turned a little red, and finally
said, "Not lately."

"Are you going to prayer meeting?" was the next question.
No, he hadn't been going to prayer meeting.

I questioned each of them in turn and discovered that

they were all failing to do what they could have done. Then I said, "As hurt as I am about your asking me to come to this kind of a meeting, I believe that God has sent me to save you from a very great danger. What you really need is a prayer meeting. You tell me that your pastor is moral and that he preaches the truth and beyond that he is the man that you called. God is the one with whom you need to discuss this situation."

Down on our knees on that dirty courthouse floor we had a prayer meeting. When it was done, I said, "I want a promise from you. This is the least that I can ask. Will you faithfully promise me to pray for your pastor every day?" I went from man to man looking him in the eye and asked the question insisting that he tell me the truth. Without exception they promised. Things began to get better right away, and it was not long before they raised the pastor's salary. When my friend finally was led from that place to another work, he went away with the real love of the congregation.

There are certain things that the deacons may expect from the pastor. They may expect him to be true to the Book and to have a character that is consonant with the message that he preaches. He will in turn expect from them their most earnest prayers and their encouragement to his ministry.

The deacon.—It is an axiom that the deacon must have a conviction about his own office. He should believe that he occupies a divinely-instituted office and that his selection by the church was the work of the Holy Spirit. In the light of that, he is to feel that he is a man signally honored among men. He is entitled to take a just and godly pride in the office that has been given him. Under no circumstances is he to be ashamed or to apologize for his office. Not only do the church and pastor have the right to ask his best, but the true deacon will feel that death would be preferable to dishonoring his office.

It is certainly true of the deacon that the character of his service will be determined by the strength of his convictions. "As he thinketh in his heart, so is he" (Prov. 23:7). For a man to fail at the point of his convictions is to defeat the whole purpose of his deaconship.

In summary, what are the obligations of the deacon to the church? First, there is an obligation to honor the good name of the church. In the second place, there is an obligation of faith (the theme of this chapter). Finally, there is the obligation of faithfulness, as a man gives himself full length to the privileges of his service.

In turn, there are some obligations of the churches to the deacons. First, they are obligated to seek God's guidance in their selection. Second, they are certainly obligated to encourage the deacons. A few kind words could change the character of a church because of that which it would do in the lives of the men so encouraged. Third, they should by all means be definite in their policies. All too often, there are no sharp corners, no clear lines of distinction regarding what the church expects to be done. Finally, most important of all, they are obligated to pray for these men as God's chosen men, his chosen servants.

IX.

THE DEACON'S HOME

And the next day we that were of Paul's company departed, and came unto Caesarea: and we entered into the house of Philip the evangelist, which was one of the seven; and abode with him. And the same man had four daughters, virgins, which did prophesy" (Acts 21:8-9).

More than twenty years had gone by since Philip had been selected by that first church at Jerusalem to be one of the seven. In the first record, it is difficult to think of these seven men as family men. They stand so splendidly alone as giants in the service of their Lord and their church. Philip, as a preaching deacon, had been responsible for the great Samaritan revival (Acts 8:5 ff). He had proclaimed Christ to these Samaritans and wrought signs before them with the result that multitudes of men and women gave heed and were baptized. They had been under the influence of a certain sorcerer, Simon, who himself also believed and was baptized, moved, as results proved, by the desire to learn the secret of Philip's ability to perform miracles.

It was also in this period that Philip had his experience with the Ethiopian eunuch, who was returning from worshipping in the temple at Jerusalem on the road to Gaza. Philip expounded to him a portion of Isaiah 53 which he had been reading aloud when Philip joined him. It possibly was during these first years of service as one of the seven that four daughters were born to Philip and to his wife. When Paul came to Caesarea on his way to Jerusalem, he spent the night in the house of Philip and his family. These girls had

119

become mature women, preachers of the gospel. The intimations of the Scripture are all good about the family life of this man that is considered one of the first deacons.

Every preacher's precious memories contain deacons' homes that have made wonderful contributions to his life. In my own experience, there was the deacon's home in the days when our children were young that was so ready to help us with the cares and responsibilities that are peculiar to young parents. How much their love meant to us and to our babies! There was the deacon's home that so graciously entertained us when I was preaching for a church "in view of a call." The years that followed made this home a tower of strength to my life. The love that existed in the family, the attitude of nine wonderful children towards their parents, the patriarchal faithfulness to the church, were wonderful blessings to me. There was the deacon's home in which I spent so many pleasant hours and in which by special request my family spent the last night of a wonderful pastorate.

Marriage and the home are of divine origin. God created man by a direct act of creation, breathed into his nostrils the breath of life so that he became a living soul, made him—unlike all the rest of creation—in the image of God. He created in man a capacity for marriage unlike the consorting of the beasts. He made man sensible for his needs of a companion and thus prepared him for Eve. Out of man God took Eve and presented her unto the man. A part of the marriage ceremony is found in the New Testament. "For this cause shall a man leave father and mother and shall cleave to his wife: and they twain shall be one flesh . . . Wherefore they are no more twain but one flesh. What therefore God hath joined together, let not man put asunder" (Matt. 19:5-6).

Such a union makes all the experiences of life joint experiences. That which changes the course of one life must of necessity and in some degree cause change in the life of the other. For a man to become a deacon in a Baptist church is to introduce in his life a new major task. Consciously or unconsciously every decision he makes will have this relationship somewhere in the background.

There is therefore nothing startling in the fact that the same Scripture which lists some of the qualifications of the deacon should also contain an admonitory word concerning his family. It would be surprising if it were absent. If this admonition goes unheeded, the effectiveness of the man's deaconship will be diminished.

"Even so must their wives be grave, not slanderers, sober, faithful in all things. Let the deacons be the husbands of one wife, ruling their children and their own houses well." (1 Tim. 3:11, 12)

There are those who want to translate the word "wives" as "women," but the context suggests the first. It is certainly consonant with this book that a wife should enter into the responsibilities and sweet promises of this office without being publicly set apart by the church in an ordination service. If a deacon has a wife, she can add much or subtract much from his deaconship. Most of us would agree that we have seen many a man who had every potentiality for being a fine deacon except that his wife was not sympathetic and helpful in the midst of his responsibility. This means, of course, that he does not bear the relationship towards the home that the Scripture enjoins.

TWO SPECIAL CASES

The unmarried deacon.—Must a man be married in order to be a deacon? No. The Scripture does not say at all that marriage is required for the office of deacon. There is no suggestion that a wife is a prerequisite for ordination to the office. It is said that he must be the husband of one wife, if married. The emphasis is upon the fact that there is only one. It is generally accepted in Baptist churches that a man that has two living wives ought not to be selected as a deacon. Very often this excludes from the office a good, faithful, godly man that has proved himself before the church in the bonds of a second marriage. The Scripture, however, is so positive about it that it is best that the service of the man be directed into other useful channels in the life of his church. On the other hand, the unmarried man may be selected by the church, may address himself faithfully to the office, and render a very effective service to the church as a deacon.

That is not quite the end of it, however. The single deacon has special responsibilities and should bear certain things in mind if he is to accept the office. Should he marry, he will be spiritually obligated to consider his deaconship and whether or not the one chosen will accept the primary obligation that is the vow of his heart. He must consider whether or not his prospective bride will bring to his office the things which God expects of a deacon's wife. His vow was not made unto men but unto God and was a vow for life. It involves the most sacred things in life and calls a man to consider well what his marriage will mean to his service.

A young woman who is planning to become a deacon's wife should also consider some things. What kind of a deacon has the prospective husband made in the church where he serves? This will really be important. The very fact that he is a deacon will have a decided effect on the kind of home that he will have. His vow towards the deaconship will make both a demand upon, and a contribution to, his home. It will bring added joy and love into it. It would be advisable for a young woman making such a choice to give adequate consideration to what it means to be a deacon and to the things that are expected of a man so dedicated to the Lord.

In one church that I served, there was a young man about twenty-five years of age, a college graduate, a certified public accountant, who was one of the most capable and gifted young men that I have ever seen. No one could have been more faithful in his church than was he. He could sing, he could teach, he could do many things effectively for the Lord and loved to do them. After much consideration it was decided by the church that he should be asked to serve as a deacon though he was not married. With a full consideration of the office he accepted and was ordained upon the authority of the church. Things that are found in this discussion about the deacon's wife were said in the ordination. Later he met the young woman who was to become his wife. She was not a Baptist but a Roman Catholic. Undoubtedly he felt sure that that was a thing that could be worked out after marriage. The tragedy is, though, that his marriage ended his usefulness as a deacon and in fact, finally divorced him from the faith and the service that had been the glory of his youth.

The wife of another denomination.—The question is sometimes raised about whether a man whose wife belongs to another evangelical denomination can be a deacon in a Baptist church. There is nothing in the scriptural instructions concerning the office to indicate that this would bar a man from service. There are many examples to be found of deacons' wives that belong to other denominations who by their sympathy, their understanding, and their co-operation make wonderful contributions to the effectiveness of a man's deaconship. It does not have to be a fatal bar to a man's usefulness as a deacon. Nevertheless, it is not at all ideal and will present some unusual problems to the man who seeks to serve under those conditions. It should be expected that the wife will be as faithful to her church as he is to his. This can often become a great strain in a home, particularly when children come into its life. It can easily become an area in the life of the home that has a closed door, not subject to discussion. Such an area is never healthy for the love of the home.

The non-Baptist wife of a man that has been selected as a Baptist deacon should realize that the things that are incumbent upon other deacons' wives also are necessary for her if she is to make an effective contribution to her husband's service. The manner of life, the degree of understanding, and the sympathetic encouragement in the work are all essential for the wife who wants to do her part. She, too, will do well to seek to have an understanding of what this office is in a Baptist church, an understanding of the significance of the lifelong vow which her husband has taken in his heart. Such an understanding will help to remove a difficulty.

THE QUALIFICATIONS OF THE DEACON'S WIFE

Not a slanderer.—In discussing the qualifications of the deacon, it was said that there are three negative qualifications, namely, not to be greedy of filthy lucre, not to be given to much wine, and not to be doubletongued. There is only one negative consideration mentioned as a qualification for a deacon's wife: she is not to be a slanderer. This is not to be found concerning the deacon or the preacher but is reserved for the deacon's wife. Consider carefully this word "slanderer." The Greek word is *diabolos,* and this is the only place in the New Testament where it is translated this way. Thirty-five times it is translated "devil." Twice it is translated "false accuser." The Holy Spirit says that the deacon's wife is not to be the things this word describes.

The word "devil" means a false accuser. In the passage in the Book of Job where Satan comes in among the children of God, he is represented in this role. He accused Job to God, saying in effect, "If you really knew Job, you would know that he is not faithful to you." He slyly suggested that if he himself had Job's cattle and sheep and family and position and other things, he would also look like a righteous man. The things that follow prove him the liar that he is. One of his chief activities is lying accusation.

The deacon's wife is one of those women in the church that has the privilege of communication. There are few deacons and no preachers that can avoid going home and talking to their wives about church troubles. That is natural, but it is a good springboard from which a man or woman can go out to make false accusations about other people. It is said of a deacon that he is not to be doubletongued and of the deacon's wife that she is to have a careful tongue. Surely there is nothing that can destroy a deacon's usefulness more quickly than a wife who has a careless tongue or a malicious tongue. One expositor has suggested, "While men are more prone than women to be doubletongued, women are more prone than men to be slanderers."

The fact that no other negatives are included in the account suggests the seriousness of this one warning. Most pastors would agree that the most serious sin, as nearly as the Bible makes a comparative record of sin, is the sin of the tongue. It is significant to me that James, the pastor, is the one that wrote the chapter about the tongue. The sin that damns is unbelief, but the sin that destroys the usefulness of a Christian is the sin of a careless and malicious tongue. It reaches deeper into the place where people live and into the place where men ought to meet God than any other sin.

Grave.—There are positive qualifications, to be sure. The deacon's wife is to be "grave," the same word that is used about the deacon. It means to be "venerated for character." There is enough stability in her character, worthwhileness in her personal bearing, and genuineness in her faith to attract the respect of people in the church.

Sober.—The deacon's wife is to be sober. The generally accepted meaning of the term is represented by the word "temperate." To let this apply, as do some, to abstinence from wine is to limit the meaning all too much. In fact, it is said that the preacher is "not given to wine." This would not be necessary if the meaning of this other word is limited simply to that area.

Surely this is to be the description of a life well lived, a life lived in perfect balance, a life that abstains from the hurtful and the harmful and a life that treats the good things of life with a moderation that God would approve. A deacon's wife who desires that her husband should be the kind of deacon that he ought to be in rendering the most effective service can contribute to that service by carefully cultivating the qualities that God has set forth in this passage concerning the deacon's wife.

THE DEDICATED WIFE

A most difficult requirement of a deacon's wife, one that requires a great degree of personal dedication, is that she be willing to consecrate and contribute her husband to his work as a deacon. One of the first things that a woman learns after marriage is that she must share this husband of hers with a vocational responsibility to which he is called. Often it is very difficult for her to accept the fact that there are interests in her husband's life with which she must share him. He is in business. He has to go out into a competitive world to make a living. She expects him then to get up in the morning to go and do that thing which his vocation demands. She understands that business is going to take certain vitality and energy out of him. The sooner that is accepted as the pattern of a home, the greater the chance is that the home will find happiness in sharing.

When this matter of being a deacon comes into her husband's life, there is a new lesson to be learned all over again. This is no thirty-day responsibility which he has accepted but a way of life and a willingness to serve which he has entered for life. There will be inescapable demands made upon him because he is a deacon. If a deacon's wife should read the above discussion of what a deacon ought to do, she might very well believe that she will never see her husband again. The emphasis here is that a deacon's wife must be willing to share her husband with the church and its service for the glory of God.

Not only must she accept the fact that there is necessary time to be spent at the office or on his job, but now time will actually be demanded for the work which he is to do in his church as a deacon. Deacons' meetings are to be attended, special capacities of service will be discovered, special services will be required, and many meetings will need to be attended to which she will accompany him.

In all of this, the deacon's wife can contribute a sympathetic, prayerful encouragement as she dedicates her husband to God. An experienced deacon's wife will have discovered already that her husband comes home from the deacons' meeting on some occasions when he needs somebody's encouragement. He is going to come home from many church meetings when he needs the prayerful encouragement of somebody that loves him. It is no time to sit down and have a good critical talk fest about the shortcomings of the membership. It is the time to talk about the blessings of the Lord and the privileges of serving God and how well God has wrought and how greatly he has blessed, a time to remember the trials through which he has safely led. Those are the hours when the need is to talk about good things.

One of the sweetest truths to us as Christians is that the more we give our loved ones to God the more we possess them. The spirit of the Word promises the deacon's wife that in giving her husband to this office in the right fashion, in not being jealous of the demands that it makes on his time and the things that are called forth from him as he makes it a primary responsibility of life, God will in turn make a contribution to her love that is not of this world.

DEACONS RULE THEIR HOUSES

This is a rather ambitious requirement for a people that live in a day that emphasizes the equality of the sexes. If there is a passage of scripture in the New Testament that would make me wonder about Paul's marital status, it would be this one. Not many preachers put the word "obey" into marriage ceremonies. We are too realistic for that. What does it mean when it requires that a deacon should be a man that rules his own house? Is the emphasis upon the rule or upon the well? It is upon both.

Recall the opening Scripture of this chapter that tells of a deacon who had a wife and four daughters. What chance did he have? I have a wife and one daughter and do well to hold my own. How is a man actually going to conform to this requirement? It is perfectly obvious, I think, that none of the ugly, harsh things that this word "rule" commonly suggests are to be found in any marriage relationship or in the home of the deacon.

A man is to rule his own house well by total love in the giving of himself to his family. This means time spent with the family. It means comradeship. It means companionship. It means sharing the bitter and the sweet. It means love, repeatedly expressed by word and deed. A deacon ought to make a better husband because of the sweetness and privilege of kingdom responsibility. The spiritual privileges that are accorded him as a servant of the church and a servant of God should be reflected in the home in a deeper, more wonderful relationship. The capacity which God will give him in his office of deacon to care for the church membership, to care about more people, to be concerned about their spiritual growth, their spiritual welfare, will increase his capacity for love in the area of the family. The dependence of the deacon upon his Heavenly Father introduces the principle of will into the family that is essentially needed. If a deacon cannot rule his own household by love, he cannot rule it at all.

The deacon and his wife who have the kind of home they should have—where each one, as part of the contract, has made his own dedication and committal to God—will find that there is a joint reward. They have a home that has God's protection built around it. God has special fences that he erects around the lives of the families of his servants. This does not necessarily mean freedom from trial or suffering— witness the original seven. It does mean that in the sorrows and shadows that life brings, even to a deacon's or a preacher's family, there will be the presence, power, and victories of our Lord. God makes a special promise to a home that is built upon a dedicated life and a committal to service.

The obligations that rest upon the husband and wife in the deacon's home are not as forbidding as they may sound. Actually, they are an admission into a special privilege of God. An extra note of sweetness and a quality of permanence are introduced into the home genuinely dedicated to God. This kind of home is not just a qualification for the deaconate. It is something that a deacon needs for the good of his own soul and for the good of the kingdom. There is also a promise from God that this sort of home relationship is within the reach of a man who accepts into his life the privilege and responsibility of the deacon's office.

The children reared in this atmosphere of privilege will "rise up and call him blessed." Godly respect and love will cause these children to adopt higher standards to live selectively. Theirs is a "goodly heritage."

X.

THE WAGES OF A DEACON

Stephen, whose name means "crown," is by far the most distinguished of those seven who were first selected to serve the church at Jerusalem. He probably was one of those Jews, known as Hellenists (the "Grecians" of Acts 6:1), who had been influenced by Greek culture. There is an unauthenticated tradition that both he and Philip were members of the seventy. Upon his selection in Acts 6, it was immediately evident that he was well qualified to become the foremost defender of the Christian way.

His very ability brought him into difficulty. The Pharisees found themselves utterly helpless before the force of his witness and the logic of his reasoning. His acquaintance with the Old Testament, in which they themselves were so well versed, was in itself a disconcerting thing. The more successfully he met their arguments against Christianity, the greater grew their rage. The sermon which Stephen preached when he was arraigned before the Sanhedrin is one of the most fully recorded sermons in all the New Testament.

It was the mad fury of a mob that finally took his life. When his enemies could do nothing with his arguments or his preaching, they took matters into their own hands. The thing that followed was very comparable to a modern lynching. There is every reason to believe that Stephen knew that the hour of his death had arrived. Even before the first stone struck his body, he recognized that such fury as belonged to his enemies could be answered only by his death. Contrary to Roman law and order, they seized Stephen without awaiting sentence against him. He was stoned to death, the punishment prescribed in Mosaic law for a blasphemer. Jewish legal forms were observed to the extent that Stephen was taken outside the city for his stoning.

Stephen died as he had lived, a faithful witness to the Christ whom he had acknowledged. His two last utterances are shouts of triumph: "Lord Jesus, receive my spirit" (Acts 7:59), and "Lord, lay not this sin to their charge" (Acts 7:60). In thinking of what happened to Stephen, does it seem that being a deacon is really worth while? Such self-examination requires that a man also remember others who have given their lives for their faith in Jesus, a long list of martyrs indeed.

How legitimate is the profit motive in kingdom service? It is always difficult for the Christian to talk about rewards, for all must remember that they are debtors to grace. Each one, like Paul, sees himself again and again as "the chief of sinners" by remembering the price Christ paid for him. Even the rewards of Christian service are all determined by grace.

There is a great deal that God has put into his Book about the future of his servants. The promises for tomorrow are carefully treasured by the believing heart. Even death is a profit transaction, "to die is gain." Undoubtedly the purpose of all these promises of God concerning tomorrow is to beckon the Christian on, to urge fuller effort, and to encourage in the midst of struggle.

In the case of deacons, hard work is called for, consecration is challenged, and sacrifice is expected; but the rewards are wonderful. What wages does the office of deacon pay?

Now and again, I will hear some deacon in our church say in the midst of a particularly demanding period of service, "I believe we ought to strike for higher pay."

In equally good humor, I have always answered, "I believe that's right. I'll just recommend that we raise your wages."

A deacon's wages do not have to be reported on his statement of income to the government; but for his own good, he should give real consideration to the return that is his because he is a deacon. God plainly considers it proper to look toward the end of this matter, through the cross to the crown.

The seven.—Stephen's capable witness found an end in martyrdom. Philip is the next of the seven in being well known. The length of his service as recorded by the Scriptures was more than twenty years, and yet tradition has it that Philip, himself, became a martyr at Tralles in Asia Minor. All that is known about the others is also tradition and therefore very uncertain. Prochorus by tradition became a martyr at Antioch. Prior to his martyrdom, he had become bishop of Nicomedia. Parmenas, tradition says, was martyred at Philippi in the reign of Trajan.

The Scripture says that Nicolas was a proselyte of Antioch, suggesting that the other six probably were Jews by birth. He is accused by tradition of being the founder of the Nicolaitanes, an immoral sect in the churches of the first century which is condemned in Revelation 2:6 and 15. In fairness to Nicolas, it was entirely possible that the opinions of this sect did not come directly from his preaching. It could easily be believed that all of these seven men, godly, dedicated, and spiritual, came at last to a martyr's death. Was their deacon's office worth the price?

It is worth noting that, as far as the record goes, they were enabled to meet their hour victoriously. The "way out" from this life awaits everyone. In Christ Jesus, it is possible to have a victorious exit. There is a certain lustre and radiance that surrounds the names and lives of these deacons of yesterday in their triumphant martyrdom. Their story contains a promise of victory for deacons of other generations as they are brought face to face with life's great emergencies.

It is fair to the record to say that the man who serves God faithfully as a deacon may expect that God will provide an extra degree of victory in the trials that will come to him and extra joy as a crown.

The kingdom grows.—The Scriptures record some immediate results from the election of these first seven to the responsibility assigned to them. It is said, "The word of God increased." Was this not the very thing for which they were elected, to liberate the preachers to the work of their ministry? The word of God increased quantitatively in that there was a greater number of witnesses. It also increased qualitatively in the effectiveness of the pastor's ministry. Those deacons who have a desire to make their pastor a more able preacher, preaching with greater power and spiritual force, have a great opportunity to produce the desired result. According to the New Testament plan, nothing can do as much to multiply the effectiveness of the pulpit as a group of deacons working faithfully at the task assigned to them by the church.

"The number of the disciples multiplied in Jerusalem greatly" (Acts 6:7). Every church should be reaping a perennial harvest. The thing that took place in the Jerusalem church can take place just as well in any New Testament church. When distribution of responsibility is made according to the Scriptures and men accept their place of privilege and responsibility, the expected result is an ingathering of souls. In this passage of Scripture, the quickened tempo of march in the kingdom of God can almost be felt. So great was the revival induced by the work of these faithful seven that "a great company of the priests were obedient to the faith." The influence of a godly man reaches into high places and low. The most determined opposition can be overcome by faithful, consecrated, dedicated witnessing. All of this is within the deacon's reach and is a definite part of his wages.

The fellowship reward.—A man that is willing to serve faithfully as a deacon in a church has the reward of a fellowship with an immortal group. The writer to the Hebrews spoke of those who have gone before when he said, "They without us should not be made perfect" (11:40). This applies to the fellowship into which the deacon enters. He becomes a part of these seven noble men of the first church. All of their successors in office become a part of the heritage of every modern deacon.

How happy a man ought to be in the twentieth century to number Stephen as a part of his personal heritage in Christ Jesus, as well as the many unnamed men of the intervening centuries that have served faithfully, lived victoriously, and died triumphantly. In the more immediate past, there are those deacons that one can remember who have witnessed to others, blessed others, and challenged others by their dedication. The deacon becomes a part of them by entering the circle of their service.

I remember a father who was a plain man serving as deacon in a church to which I had been called. No one attended the services more regularly than he, a man of prayer and compassion and faithfulness. He was a tower of strength to his pastor. In the meetings of the deacons, he could be depended upon to take the spiritual view that great faith was essential to great success. In church affairs, his standards of life were those that befitted a dedicated man.

Now his son, my friend, has been ordained to be a deacon in the same church. He serves as the Sunday school superintendent. The life in his home is the life of a dedicated family. His service is readily given to every activity of the church. The things that he stands for are the things that a New Testament church holds up as the Christian standard. There are many father-son combinations just like this one. One generation has produced another worthy to be set aside

by the church as deacon. Could there be better wages than
these? Not only a fellowship of a family tie but the fellowship of a divinely ordained service is reward beyond measure.

The good degree.—This is a degree-conscious generation.
After their names, men proudly display letters which indicate their eminence in training or achievement in the eyes of
their fellows. Perhaps in the light of the biblical expression
that men who "have used the office of deacon well purchase
to themselves a good degree" (1 Tim. 3:13), it might be possible to create a new degree, say the "D. F. D.," "Doctor of
Faithful Deaconing." In view of the requirement, I believe
that a man will find that this is more than a two- or four-
year course. In fact, no degree could be more deserved than
one accorded to a man who has devoted his life to demon-
strating that the biggest thing for him is the service assigned
him by God. A man may have a higher, nobler end in view
than the achieving of a degree, but a degree is recognition of
the fact that he has devoted himself faithfully to a high
ideal.

The word "degree" in the passage in Timothy means
"threshold" or "step." It is used particularly of a grade of
dignity and wholesome influence in the church. It does not
necessarily imply an advance in rank but an assured position
in the esteem of fellow Christians. Among the many who
possess the same rank, whether in church or state, some gain
standing from their character and abilities that others do not
have. When first elected to the office, they are like many
many others in the church. As they begin to serve, they almost visibly increase in spiritual stature.

We elected a young man as a deacon in our church. He
was college trained and had no reason to feel any sense of
inferiority in the presence of his fellows. It was quite evident, however, in the first deacons meetings that he attended

that he had every reluctance to express an opinion before those who had served longer in the office. He quietly accepted the tasks that were assigned to him and faithfully performed them. In every meeting of the group, he seemed to increase in stature and confidence. He remains a quiet, modest, faithful, dedicated young man; and yet it has come to be that his opinions are invited and respected. He has advanced a grade, he has taken a step forward, he has crossed a threshold; in other words, he is on the way to his good degree.

In churches large and small, men are elected to the office of deacon that have not had equal secular preparation. Some of them are self-made men having had little formal education. It is quite true of all of them, however, that if they faithfully serve in the office of deacon, they develop in spiritual effectiveness in the eyes of the church. This growth indicates that they are moving forward step by step towards the degree that is promised the man who faithfully serves.

Great boldness in the faith.—One of the words most often used of Jesus in his ministry is "boldness." It had to do with his bearing before those that were against him. Nothing intimidated our Lord's word. It was said of the early apostles that they spoke the word of God with boldness, the same characteristic that had been found in Jesus, for it was the result of their fellowship with Christ. Now the scriptures say of the New Testament deacons that they may have "great boldness in the faith" (1 Tim. 3:13). This has been defined as "a confident public expression of the faith, such as would belong to an experienced Christian who had gained a good standing and in consequence had no temptation to be doubletongued." That may be just a little long and confused, but it suggests that these men by their faithfulness had lost all sense of the apologetic, and courageously and positively presented their testimony for the Lord.

How many churches are handicapped by timid men? There are so few that will speak confidently, with the assurance that is born of experienced Christian service, and will boldly launch their programs of faith. This quality is not lightly bestowed by the Lord. It is for the faithful servant, the tried and experienced deacon, the man who has been willing to accept the full responsibility of his office for the delight that is found in faithfully serving Jesus Christ.

Put it like this. The greatest thing in this world is to be a Christian, to be able to say confidently, "I know whom I have believed." Within that Christian experience, the next greatest privilege is to be a loyal, faithful member of a New Testament church. The blessings of God upon such a membership are almost innumerable. Third, within the membership of a New Testament church, there can be no greater privilege than to be chosen of the church under the wisdom of God to be a Baptist deacon. It challenges the man so selected to make the best and wisest investment of his life.

In my first pastorate after seminary days, the outstanding man in my church was one who had served as deacon in the church for almost fifty years. His position in the church was due to no self-seeking on his part. He had no "bossism" complex nor desire to control. In fact he was almost a timid man, so retiring was he and so modest in every respect. He was quick to listen to the opinions of others, and most willing to follow the plan which someone else had suggested and which others approved. He could, however, on a matter that he considered sacred, rise and speak courageously for his Lord. When he did, what he said settled the matter, so respected was he by the church.

How had he achieved such stature? It was the result of years in which he had faithfully done his best to serve his Lord in an office which God himself had planned. He was a soul-winner, a true brother to every member of that church;

and there were no high stations and low in the love that was in his heart. He was a source of unfailing strength to his pastor through all his years of Christian witnessing. In that little county seat town, his shadow had grown longer and longer. The day came that God called him home. It is a never-to-be-forgotten memory how the people came and filled the church, flowed out onto the lawns, and stood by reverently remembering with gratitude to God the life of a man who had faithfully served. Could a man better invest his life than by simply taking a vow to God that by his help he will be the deacon that is needed in a world like this?